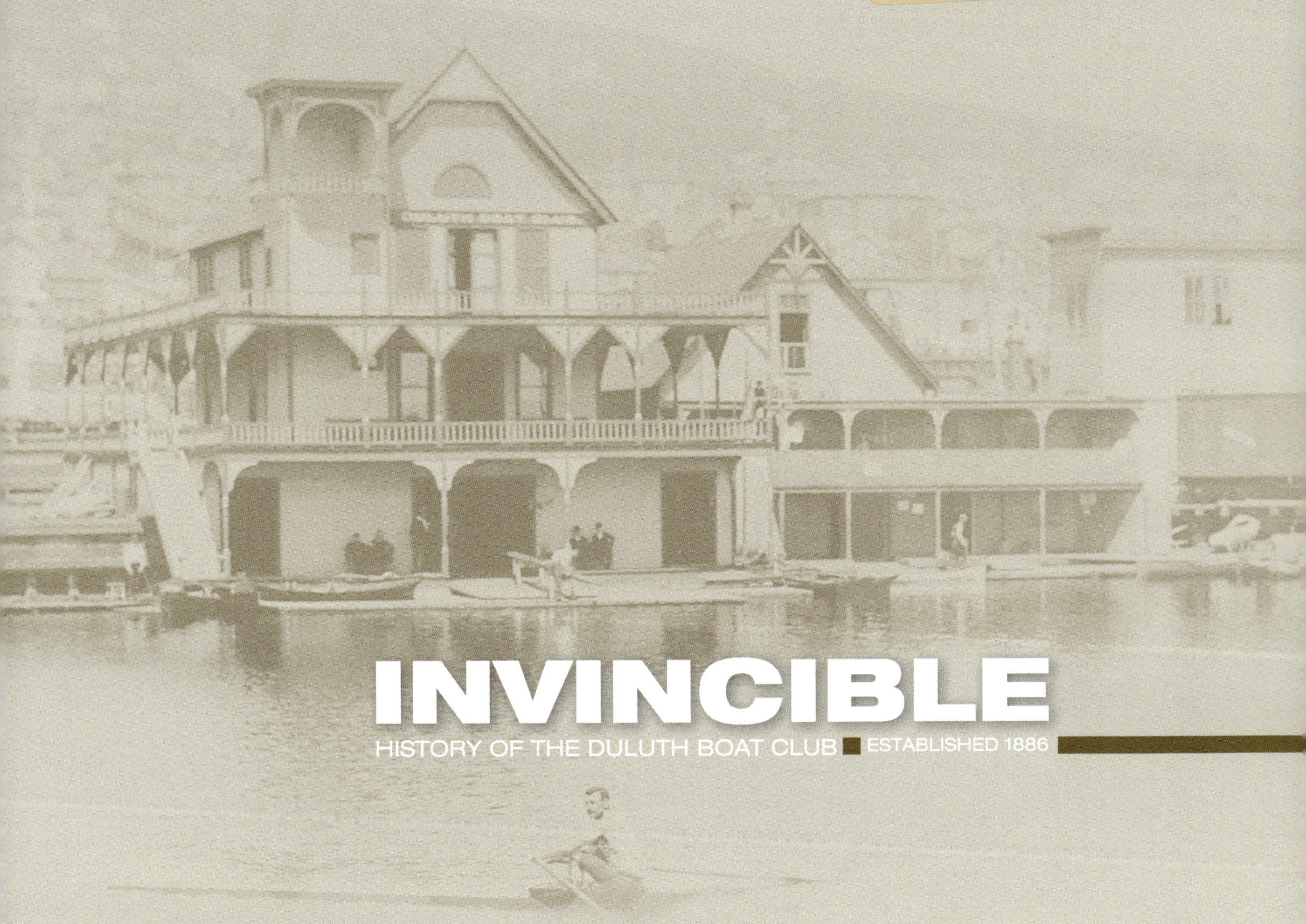

INVINCIBLE
HISTORY OF THE DULUTH BOAT CLUB | ESTABLISHED 1886

SPONSORED BY THE ST. LOUIS COUNTY HISTORICAL SOCIETY THROUGH THE GENEROSITY OF MAX RHEINBERGER, JR.

506 WEST MICHIGAN STREET ■ DULUTH, MN 55802 ■ PHONE: 218-733-7580 ■ FAX: 218-733-7585
WEBSITE: WWW.THEHISTORYPEOPLE.ORG ■ MAIN E-MAIL: HISTORY@THEHISTORYPEOPLE.ORG

THE DONNING COMPANY
PUBLISHERS

INVINCIBLE
HISTORY OF THE DULUTH BOAT CLUB ■ ESTABLISHED 1886

By Michael J. Cochran

Dedication

Dedicated to the late Henning Peterson, whose many stories of the Duluth Boat Club inspired the author to write this book.

Copyright © 2008 by St. Louis County Historical Society and Michael J. Cochran

All rights reserved, including the right to reproduce this work in any form whatsoever without permission in writing from the publisher, except for brief passages in connection with a review. For information, please write:

The Donning Company Publishers
184 Business Park Drive, Suite 206
Virginia Beach, VA 23462

Steve Mull, General Manager
Barbara Buchanan, Office Manager
Pamela Koch, Senior Editor
Jennifer Penaflor, Graphic Designer
Derek Eley, Imaging Artist
Scott Rule, Director of Marketing
Tonya Hannink, Marketing Coordinator

Steve Mull, Project Director

Library of Congress Cataloging-in-Publication Data

Cochran, Michael J.
  Invincible : history of the Duluth Boat Club / by Michael J. Cochran.
    p. cm.
  Includes bibliographical references.
  ISBN 978-1-57864-495-7 (hard cover : alk. paper) -- ISBN 978-1-57864-496-4 (soft cover : alk. paper)
  1. Duluth Boat Club (Minn.) 2. Rowing clubs--Minnesota--Duluth--History. I. Title.
  GV793.C63 2008
  797.12'309776771--dc22
                              2008008142

Printed in the United States of America at Walsworth Publishing Company

contents

foreword **6**
BY CRAIG LINCOLN

acknowledgments **7**

introduction **9**

the early years: 1886–1900 **10**

the glory years: 1900–1926 **22**

JULIUS BARNES

the invincible era **52**

JACK KELLY

PAUL COSTELLO

JACK BERESFORD

WALTER HOOVER

decline and fall **96**

born again: an epilogue **104**

about the author **128**

foreword

One day several years ago, the coach of the Duluth Rowing Club introduced me to some members who had rowed competitively at national and international levels. It seemed improbable to me, having recently moved to this small city at the tip of Lake Superior.

As time went by, the improbable story of Duluth's watersports history became believable.

When Mike Cochran, one of the rowers, began sharing drafts and photos of this book, that story went from believable to incredible. For a period of time, the elite rowers of the original Duluth Boat Club—founded largely as a social club—dominated the sport of rowing. They were truly invincible. It was enough to make the *New York Times* stand up and take notice.

The club's coaches developed innovative training regimes and required a lifestyle so disciplined that it seems unbearable. The rowers rode trains to the biggest competitions in the nation, where they beat the best from the biggest cities.

Perhaps it wasn't as surprising to Duluthians back then, as their city was booming. It seems the "Zenith City," as its boosters called it, was destined to eclipse Chicago in size and power, and as part of that zeitgeist, its rowers were destined to win every race.

But Duluth crashed in the 1920s, and the Duluth Boat Club was one victim. As memories faded, the Boat Club's accomplishments became something Duluthians mentioned only in clichés, such as "The Invincible Four." Mike Cochran's book brings out the full life of the program, a story that has lessons and inspiration for any competitor.

It's a story of audacity, of how a small community's willpower, drive, and belief can create a world-class program; a story of how dedication, discipline, and innovation can make it possible for any athlete to compete with the best; and, sadly, how hard it is to sustain that level of success in a small town.

But you'll also learn that although the original Duluth Boat Club disbanded, watersports haven't died in Duluth.

The city is home to internationally competitive rowers, sailors, and paddlers. It has a superb community sailing program open to all, no matter what their financial capability, and an exceptional program to introduce watersports to people with disabilities.

People like Mike Cochran are key to keeping that tradition alive. I consider myself lucky to be a part of bringing the Duluth Boat Club back to life.

CRAIG LINCOLN

acknowledgments

The publication of this book was made possible by a generous grant from the estate of the late Max Rheinberger, Jr. Max was the son of the great Duluth rower Max Rheinberger, Sr., one of the Invincible Four. Max Jr. also served on the Board of Directors of the Duluth Rowing Club and, through his estate, left a generous donation to the DRC. I am very grateful that Mrs. Max Rheinberger Jr. and the St. Louis County Historical Society selected me to author this work.

Pat Maus from the Northeast Minnesota Historical Center was indispensable in obtaining images of the Duluth Boat Club. The Northeast Minnesota Historical Center, archives of the St. Louis County Historical Society, has a very extensive and impressive collection of regional historical information and has a wealth of wonderful images and documents from the Duluth Boat Club. Pat's extensive historical knowledge and advice have been a tremendous help in assembling this story.

JoAnne Coombe, the executive director of the St. Louis County Historical Society, has been extremely supportive of this work in every regard. She contracted for the book to be published by the Donning Company and engaged the entire staff of the Historical Society to assist in this project. Susan Schwanekamp and Julie Bolos were both involved with the finances for the project and are also deeply involved in marketing the book. Milissa Brooks-Ojibway Brooks from the St. Louis County Historical Society made a rich assortment of Duluth Boat Club artifacts available for photographing, which was performed very ably and professionally by Bruce Ojard Photographics. All of the St. Louis County Historical Society staff members have been very helpful and kind with their advice and encouragement.

This book started as a manuscript that was hand-typed with an old-fashioned typewriter thirty-five years ago. Jeanne Kruze retyped the entire manuscript in Microsoft Word, which served for many years as the unpublished history of the Duluth Boat Club and made my task of writing this book far less laborious.

There were many people who provided information and/or images for this book, including David Bjorkman, Walter Hoover Jr., Mrs. William Coventry, Walker Jamar Jr., Randy and Jan Newburg, Joseph Korman, Jerry Paulson, and Laura Jacobs, archivist of the Lake Superior Maritime Collections of the Jim Dan Hill Library at the University of Wisconsin, Superior.

My friend Craig Lincoln reviewed my rough draft and gave me professional advice. He also kindly agreed to write the foreword to this book. Many friends from the Duluth Rowing Club helped find material for the epilogue on the current Duluth Rowing Club and Duluth Boat Club, especially Pete Olson, Craig Lincoln, and Tom Rauschenfels. Sport Graphics was very kind to permit their photographs to be used in this book.

I hope you will agree that the Donning Company has done a splendid job of assembling the text and images that I provided into the book that you are now reading. I would particularly like to thank the book designer, Jennifer Penaflor, and the editor, Pamela Koch, for their work on this project. This is Jennifer's first book, and she did an awesome cover design. I couldn't be more pleased.

Finally, I would like to thank and acknowledge my wife Diane, who very patiently supported me during the past year while I neglected nearly all home maintenance responsibilities and used our family vacation time to work on this book. I am a very lucky guy.

introduction

Invincible is a history of the Duluth Boat Club, which includes a period when the oarsmen of the Duluth Boat Club completely dominated North American rowing. There was one group of four men who were never defeated in twenty-two elite races and were named the "Invincible Four." The Duluth Boat Club also included a young man who became single sculling champion of the world and an international celebrity. This all happened at a time when amateur rowing was closely followed by the general public and reported in all major newspapers. The stories of these rowing races were carried on the front pages of the *New York Times*, the *Philadelphia Enquirer*, the *Boston Globe*, and the *Times* of London.

The Duluth Boat Club was much more than just a rowing organization. It was a social club providing a nearly unimaginable array of water recreation. By 1909, the Duluth Boat Club was referring to itself as the greatest water sports organization in the world, and it later grew even larger. A claim to be the greatest in the world is difficult to prove, but when one comprehends the many hundreds of members, the fabulous events, the everyday programs, vast assets, and incomparable athletic record of the Duluth Boat Club, there is little reason to doubt the assertion. The glory of the Duluth Boat Club encompassed much more than athletics, and the word "Invincible" also describes a feeling that Duluthians once had about their community that they proudly proclaimed to be the "Zenith City of the Unsalted Seas."

Today, the existence of such an eminent organization in a small midwestern city like Duluth, Minnesota, seems very improbable. The historical context of Duluth around the turn of the century explains how this happened. The burgeoning economy and rapidly growing population of Duluth created the conditions for the founding of the club, while the vision, leadership, and financial contributions of a dynamic and renowned individual brought the Duluth Boat Club to world prominence.

The greatness of the Duluth Boat Club only lasted for a period of a little more than two decades before it went out of existence. Perhaps the club became so great it was bound to crash, like Icarus flying too close to the sun. Please read and wonder.

CHAPTER 1

the early years
1886–1900

The history of Duluth, Minnesota, does not extend back many years previous to the founding of the Duluth Boat Club in 1886. Thirty-five years before this event, few people even anticipated that a town would ever exist in the wild hills at the head of Lake Superior. In 1853, there was only one white man living among the Ojibwa in the area that would later become the city of Duluth.[1]

This photograph of early downtown Duluth was taken around 1870. Early Duluth had the pungent character one might expect from a small, fast-growing pioneer town deep in the wilderness. An early settler, Fred W. Smith, described the Duluth of 1869 as being "haphazard, scraggly, repellent, a mixture of Indian trading post, seaport, railroad construction camp and gambling resort, altogether wild, rough, uncouth and frontier-like." Mr. Smith stated, "The town was filling up with the roughest element of the country, gambling was the main business pursuit of the bulk of the population, and murder their amusement."[3] Photograph by William Henry Illingworth circa 1870.

From the collection of the Minnesota Historical Society Loc # MS2.9 DU1 p61

The permanent growth of Duluth did not commence until 1867, with the beginning of the construction of the Lake Superior and Mississippi River Railroad, which extended from Saint Paul to Duluth. There was a rush of people in late 1869 through early 1870, and in just six months, Duluth grew from fourteen families to 3,500 inhabitants.[2]

Duluth was boosted by Jay Cooke's Northern Pacific Railroad, begun in 1870, the same year that Duluth was granted a city charter. But when Mr. Cooke's railroad failed in 1873, it caused a nationwide panic, which had a particularly great

CHAPTER 1: THE EARLY YEARS 1886–1900

This colorized postcard from Duluth Photo Engraving shows Superior Street in downtown Duluth in 1871.

From the personal collection of the author

effect on Duluth, the population of which was almost instantly reduced from 5,000 to 2,500. The immediate outcome of the panic was quite negative. Duluth was even forced to repudiate its enfranchisement as a city in 1879, when the municipal government became bankrupt through failure to pay off its bonds. Duluth reverted to the status of a village for over a decade.[4] However, this national financial crisis eventually forced people out of the jobless cities into primitive areas such as Duluth, which began to grow again, led by the region's timber, iron ore, and shipping industries.

Many who moved into Duluth during this period were poor immigrants, but the sudden growth in population and commerce made a disproportionate number of Duluthians extremely wealthy. The booming industries of timber, wheat, shipping, and iron ore made men rich, but fortunes were also being made in other areas of commerce, such as real estate and banking. Real estate valuations were two and one-half times greater in 1886 than in 1885.[5]

Not everyone became wealthy. During this period of American history, there was a great income disparity between socio-economic classes. While great wealth was generated on the Iron Range, miners worked for ten cents per hour and worked ten hours daily to make a dollar a day.[6]

By the 1880s, Duluth was becoming much less primitive, and the wealthy families that had the luxury of free time began to develop the entertainment, amusements, and recreation enjoyed by the wealthy in the older, larger cities. In 1883, a magnificent opera house was opened in downtown Duluth and began hosting the finest dramatic and troupe performers of the day. However, the natural recreation that one normally associates with northern Minnesota was undeveloped. Loggers had stripped the immediate area of its majestic pines, leaving the hills a litter of stumps. The many lakes to

An engraving of the Grand Opera House in Duluth, which opened in 1883. It was located at Fourth Avenue West and Superior Street.

From the collection of the Minnesota Historical Society Loc # MS3.1 DU3.1 p4

DULUTH.—THE GRAND OPERA HOUSE.

11

The first clubhouse of the Duluth Boat Club was an imposing building located at Seventh Avenue West on the Northern Pacific slip. This undated photograph shows a single sculler in front of the club. He is believed to be one of the professional scullers who competed for prize money in the large regatta hosted by the Duluth Boat Club in 1890. The building was built and opened in 1887.

NEMHC 52386 b32af13

the north were virtually inaccessible since the roads leading to them were mostly rough logging roads. The formation of the Duluth Boat Club was an attempt to fill this recreational void, for those who could afford recreation.

Among those seeking a hobby were Charles H. Eldridge and Frederick W. Smith, prominent attorneys, who took it upon themselves to organize a club devoted to the gentlemanly sports of rowing and sailing. Through their efforts, the Duluth Boat Club was officially incorporated on July 10, 1886. Including Smith and Eldridge, there were twenty-eight charter members who elected H. W. Pearson as their first president.[7]

The newly founded Duluth Boat Club was a rather refined and exclusive organization, as one can readily infer from reading the *Articles of Incorporation, Rules, Regulations and By-Laws of the Duluth Boat Club, 1887*. The membership fee of $50.00, along with quarterly dues of $2.50, would have discouraged those earning a dollar a day from trying to join. Money alone, however, would not assure a person of a chance to become a member. The membership process was designed to reject any applicants who might prove to be socially undesirable.

CHAPTER 1: THE EARLY YEARS 1886–1900

A person seeking Duluth Boat Club membership was required to submit a written application to the club secretary, giving such personal information as his occupation and address. The application had to be endorsed by two Duluth Boat Club members as proposer and seconder. The secretary then presented the name to the Board of Directors, and the application would be posted on the club bulletin board at least one week prior to a meeting where membership could be voted on. Anyone having a complaint against the candidate could place it in writing before the Board of Directors at the meeting where the name was to be considered. The voting for active membership was by ballot. One negative vote postponed the decision on the application, while two negative votes rejected the application. There was also a rule that forbade Duluth Boat Club members from joining any other boating club or association.[8]

The *Articles of Incorporation* states the general purpose of the club as "the instruction and improvement of its members in rowing, sailing and physical development, and also in social culture." The impression is that the founders of the club listed these activities in the order of their priority and that the club was intended to be primarily an athletic organization.

However, it was the social aspect of the Duluth Boat Club that was to be displayed first. The occasion was the opening of the clubhouse on July 13, 1887. Although the reception celebrating this opening occurred only one year after the club was organized and chartered, it attained the distinction of being "the social event of the season," as the society columnist of the *Duluth Daily News* termed it.[9]

The description that this columnist gave of the reception provides an idea of the nature of the Duluth Boat Club at the time of its inception. The reception was an elaborate affair, with a banquet and dancing to a twelve-piece dance orchestra. Formal dress was worn, and it was said to have been "one of the 'dressiest' entertainments ever given in the city, . . . The gentlemen were resplendent in new and fashionable garments, while the ladies toilettes were the most varied, fine, and fashionable ever seen in the city at any gathering of that size."[10]

The superlatives were also extended to the catering, which was "by far the finest ever seen in Duluth." Twelve waiters served lake trout in aspic jelly, lobster salad, boned turkey, and ox tongue. Seven hundred people attended this reception.[11] One can only imagine the planning and logistics necessary to serve such sumptuous food to this large number of people during the nineteenth century.

Here, another sculler poses in front of some auxiliary buildings that were located next to the main clubhouse of the Duluth Boat Club.

NEMHC 52386 b32af13

13

A four-man crew gets underway at the Duluth Boat Club while people look on. Although competitive rowing was an important part of the Duluth Boat Club, most members joined for social and fitness activities. The first floor of the building had athletic facilities, but the second and third floors were dedicated to social space, including a billiard room, a banquet room, a reading room, and a balcony for spectators to watch harbor activity.[14] The photo is undated.

NEMHC 52386 b32af13

Architect Charles MacMillen, one of the boat club's charter members, designed the clubhouse. The building seems to have been quite worthy of the extravagant celebration that opened it. The ground floor contained the main boat room, bathrooms, gymnasium, and closets. The second floor had a billiard room, four dressing rooms, a spare room, ladies' toilette, and the main reception or reading room. The dressing rooms each contained twelve lockers, and their floors were covered with rich Brussels carpets. The reading room had a profusion of comfortable easy chairs and a variety of fancy rugs. The gaslight fixtures on this floor had delicately shaded crimped glass globes. These second-floor rooms opened onto a balcony, which ran entirely around the building. The third floor consisted of one large room, which was used for banquets and dances. There was also a balcony running entirely around the third floor. A spiral staircase connected these floors and led to a tower, which offered a fine view of the harbor, Lake Superior, and the hills behind the city. The clubhouse also boasted a number of conveniences that were by no means common in 1887. It had plumbing, gas, a hot water heater, and a telephone.[12] The telephone exchange in Duluth had just been started in 1882 with thirty subscribers.

The athletic function of the club was not forgotten. The clubhouse opened with a fleet of 33 boats, 25 of which were owned by the club, with the rest privately owned. Among the boats were two four-oar racing shells, four double racing shells, three single racing shells, seven clinker-built working shells, two duck boats, two family barges, plus skiffs and canoes that were privately owned.[13]

Just as the city of Duluth seemed to have grown practically overnight, so was the boat club born into full maturity. Only one year after being organized, the club had an elaborate facility, a complete set of equipment, and an impressive membership. On the very evening that the clubhouse was opened, the Duluth Boat Club was referred to as "the most popular, and at the same time (socially) select organization in the city."[14]

It only remained for the boat club to be admitted to a rowing association, and this was accomplished in the same year. The Duluth Boat Club was admitted to the Minnesota-Winnipeg Rowing Association, the first rowing association formed in the upper Midwest. It was started in 1885 with three member clubs, the Minnesota Boat Club (Saint Paul), the Saint Paul Boat Club, and the Winnipeg Rowing Club. The Lurline Rowing Club of Minneapolis was accepted in

CHAPTER 1: THE EARLY YEARS 1886–1900

1886. Duluth joined in 1887 and was followed by Rat Portage (Kenora, Ontario) in 1894. The Minnesota-Winnipeg Rowing Association lasted thirteen years, from 1885 to 1897, and it held annual regattas at Lake Minnetonka over an official one-and-one-half-mile course.[15]

Horse carriages bring people to an event at the Duluth Boat Club. Regattas and other activities at the Duluth Boat Club were among the most prominent events in Duluth. The photo is undated but a handwritten caption says "at the Duluth Regatta."

NEMHC 52386 b32af13

Prior to the formation of this rowing association, there was unorganized rowing in Minnesota. The Minnesota Boat Club had been incorporated in 1873. Soon after, there were also rowing clubs formed at Minneapolis, Stillwater, Brainerd, and Redwing. Oarsmen would practice together, and when they felt ready, they would challenge crews from other towns. Betting on these races promoted much enthusiasm in the towns involved.

The winners of the intermediate four in 1885. The person standing in the back is Julius H. Barnes, who would later be the guiding light and primary benefactor for the Duluth Boat Club. The other members of the crew shown in this photo are S. A. MacPhail, H. D. Ballou, and G. C. Calhoun.

From the personal collection of the author

15

Rowing was so popular before the turn of the century that the rowing theme was often used commercially. These are just a few images from the era showing how the sport of rowing had a certain cachet that was used to sell products.

Images from The Friends of Rowing History website http://www.rowinghistory.net/

LIEBIG COMPANY'S FLEISCH-EXTRACT.

Drink
Cadbury's
Cocoa

STOLLWERCK'SCHE CHOCOLADE

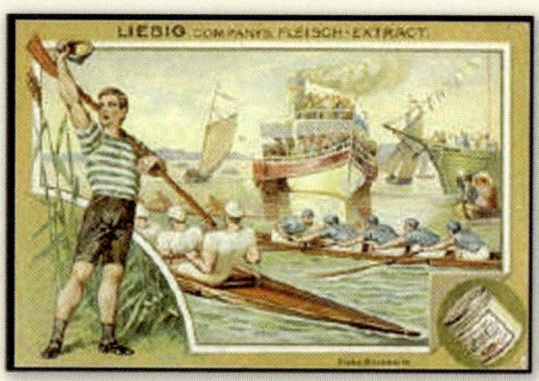

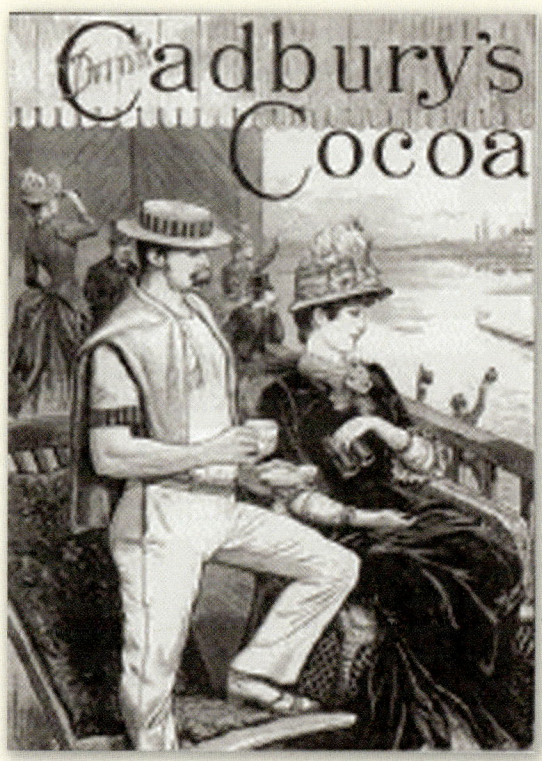

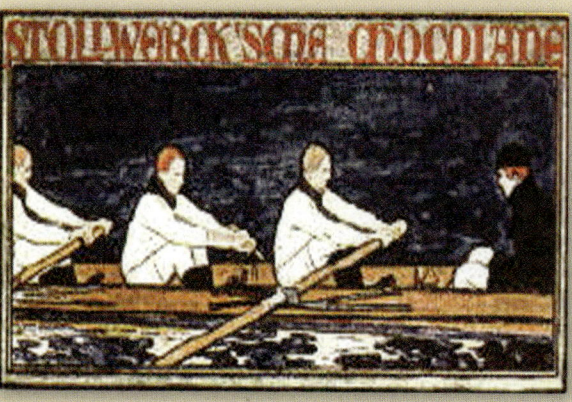

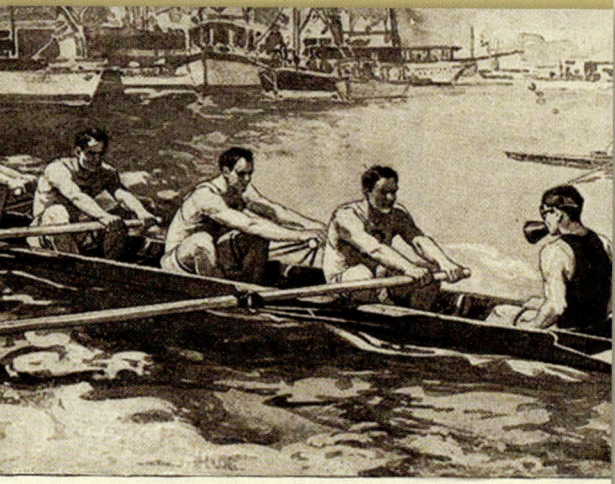

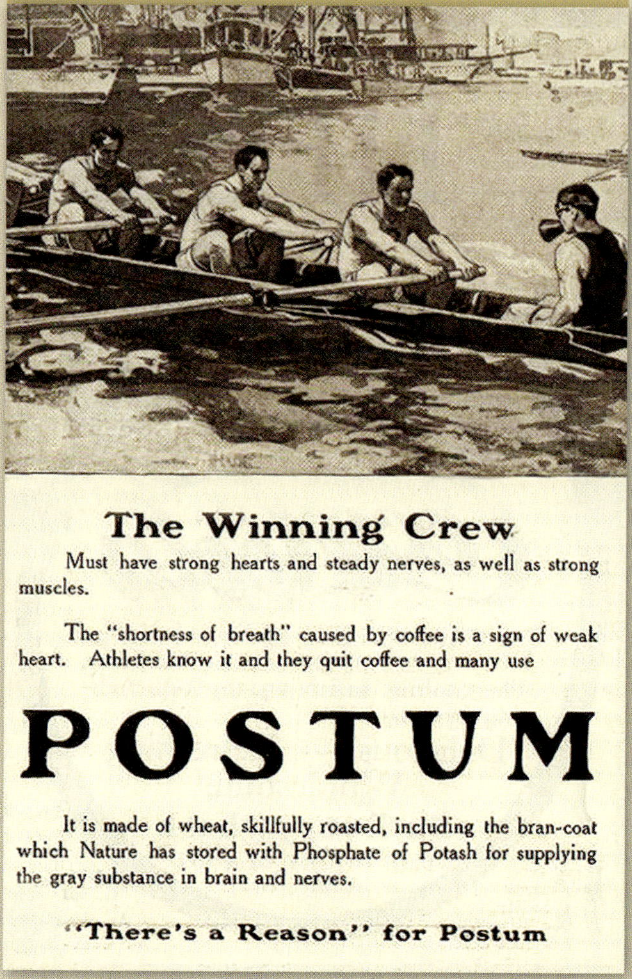
The Winning Crew
Must have strong hearts and steady nerves, as well as strong muscles.
The "shortness of breath" caused by coffee is a sign of weak heart. Athletes know it and they quit coffee and many use
POSTUM
It is made of wheat, skillfully roasted, including the bran-coat which Nature has stored with Phosphate of Potash for supplying the gray substance in brain and nerves.
"There's a Reason" for Postum

CHARTER OAK RANGES
1889. MAY. 1889.
CHARTER OAK RANGES
ROWING

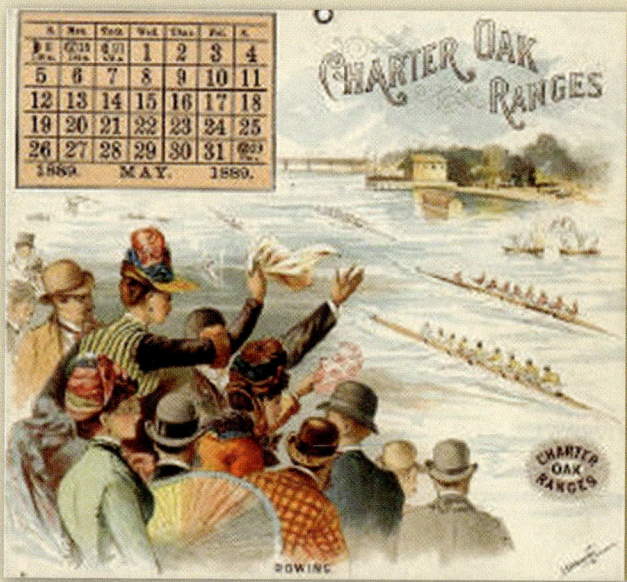

CHAPTER 1: THE EARLY YEARS 1886–1900

Rowing was an extremely popular sport during the latter part of the nineteenth century. There was both professional and amateur rowing. During the period between the end of the Civil War and the turn of the century, there were a number of famous professional oarsmen that raced for purses. These professional races were bet on in the same manner as horse races, with odds given and large sums of money bet. The gambling led to corruption, and professional rowing was tainted with suspicions of races being thrown and actual sabotage. In one famous case, a professional sculler's boat was sawn in half the night before a world championship contest. The parties of both the victim and his opponent were accused of the dirty deed as a means to avoid the big race. [Author's note: The Friends of Rowing History website has a very colorful and fascinating account of professional rowing in the nineteenth century. http://www.rowinghistory.net/professionals.htm]

While professional rowing was somewhat lowbrow, amateur rowing had an aristocratic flavor. The interest began in England, where rowing was cultivated as a gentlemen's sport. In fact, the Royal Henley Regatta officially prohibited non-gentlemen (e.g., anyone who worked with his hands) as well as professional rowers from competing. At that time, the Royal Henley Regatta was regarded as the world championship amateur rowing regatta. When amateur rowing was imported into the United States, some of this aristocratic flavor was retained. Rowing became the first intercollegiate sport in this country when Yale University challenged Harvard University to a race "to test the superiority of the oarsmen of the two colleges."[16] It was not long before rowing races (or "crew") became institutionalized in the Ivy League colleges. In the nineteenth century, an American college man was perhaps the closest comparison with the English gentleman.

In the United States, rowing did not remain exclusively an upper-class activity. As mentioned already, there were a number of small communities that had rowing clubs during this era that have since become defunct (e.g., Stillwater and Red Wing). Rowing clubs could be found in communities throughout the eastern and midwestern United States. Rowing attracted the attention of the public on many levels. There was, of course, concern for how the hometown boys fared in their local races in the region, but local newspapers, such as the *Duluth News Tribune*, would also dutifully devote much of their limited news space to reporting the large, glamorous regattas in which the elite crews participated. The annual Oxford-Cambridge and Yale-Harvard races, the U.S. national championship regatta, and the Royal Henley Regatta in England were all reported in detail.

Perhaps because rowing was an important sport in the world, the annual regattas of the Minnesota-Winnipeg Association were big events for the cities that had participating clubs. During the months preceding the annual regatta on Lake Minnetonka, the Duluth newspaper would give a weekly report on the training activities of the oarsmen, usually with optimistic predictions as to their chance of success. Win or lose, the Minnetonka regatta was always front-page news, but a victory would double or triple the amount of space devoted to the races. These races were given a detailed "play-by-play" account. It was told which crew got water first, what the various stroke ratings were that the different crews were rowing, who was ahead after a minute elapsed, which oarsmen were showing obvious signs of fatigue, which crew still looked strong and fresh at the halfway mark, and whether they were splashing water or rowing cleanly. Water conditions were described, and many more details of these races were included. The following short excerpt from one of these stories shows some of the enthusiasm shown by both the spectators and the journalists:

> Hardly a furlong had passed before the Duluths' familiarity with rough water was only too plainly evident. Inch by inch the gallant four in white forged ahead. Yell after yell went up from the launch chartered by the Duluth men. But it was evident that notwithstanding the favor that Neptune had shown the sons of the zenith city, they had no lead pipe cinch on the event . . . .
>
> The finish was an enigma to those on the judges' boat and those on the Lotus. So close was it that yells went up from every partisan except those of the Rat Portage crew. The Minnesota men were sure they had won, and the Winnipeggers and the zenith city boys with their brooms were in a similarly happy state of mind.[17]

INVINCIBLE: HISTORY OF THE DULUTH BOAT CLUB

This same crew (pictured on page 15) poses in the Duluth Harbor near the clubhouse. NEMHC S3025 B12f4

The Duluth Boat Club did win the junior four race described above, and the newspaper responded the next day by quoting the happy reactions of Duluthians who had heard the good news, and an editorial lauded the boat club and its oarsmen for their efforts.

During the 1880s and 1890s, the rowing accomplishments of the Duluth Boat Club were less than impressive, although they were up against tough competition. The Duluth oarsmen mostly competed in the junior category (which was reserved for oarsmen who had never won a race) in the Minnesota-Winnipeg association. Even in junior competition, the Duluth Boat Club was only occasionally victorious. The Duluth newspaper was also enthusiastic when describing the interclub regatta that the Duluth Boat Club held every summer. The mood of the affair was frolicsome rather than serious. The old-timers would race the youngsters, and novelty events were included, such as tub races. Despite the informality of these home regattas, the newspaper still gave them huge coverage. In 1895, this quasi-regatta received an entire front-page spread, with photographs and cartoons.[18] The story brought out occurrences that showed the regatta to be rather bush-league. The program got under way several hours late, the double race was concluded when an unfortunate pair of scullers capsized, and a four race was interrupted when a tugboat towed a mass of logs across the course. There were not enough club members in adequate condition to have a race of eight-man shells, so an eight rowed alongside a tugboat as an exhibition.

The Duluth Boat Club had to be prominent in Duluth in order for the newspaper to cover these regattas as completely as it did. By 1895, Duluth was not a small town where almost any event could make big news. Duluth's population had grown to 59,396 by this time.[19] Few other athletic activities were reported on the front page of the *Duluth News Tribune*. The front page was generally reserved for national, international, and important local news. In the case of these home regattas, it was obviously not a case of the events themselves being noteworthy. Rather, it was the participants that attracted attention, since they were the elite young men of the city.

There seems to have been only one occasion before 1900 where the Duluth Boat Club staged a huge regatta that included several amateur rowing associations and the professional rowing championship of North America. This regatta held in 1890 was the most exciting athletic event that had ever taken place in the brief history of Duluth. The regatta lasted one week, but it was the focal point for Duluthians for the entire summer. During the weeks preceding this regatta, the anticipation was intense. Nearly every day, the *Duluth Daily Tribune* ran a front-page column devoted to the regatta. The competitors were described, and worries were expressed that Duluth's hotel accommodations would prove to be insufficient for the great influx of visitors into the city that were expected to watch the races. The excitement generated by this regatta was tremendous, but the financial cost was nearly equivalent. There were purses given for the first three finishers in each of the four professional races. In the double race, for instance, first prize was $2,000, second $550, and third $350.[20] This prize money is quite significant when you realize that third prize represented the annual income of an iron miner in 1890. The boat club raised some of the prize money by sponsoring benefit plays, but it was probably contributions by affluent members of the club that produced much of the money necessary to put on this regatta. The number of out-of-town spectators was not quite as great as had been anticipated, but two thousand people did come on the trains to see the great professional singles race.[21] Despite the fact that the Duluth crews did not win any of their races, the regatta of 1890 was talked about for years afterward. The results of the 1890 Duluth Regatta were even carried in a story in the *New York Times*.

The Nushka club on a train excursion to see the Duluth Regatta in 1890.

Photograph by Truman Ward Ingersoll from the collection of the Minnesota Historical Society
Loc # GT5.4 p1

This interesting photo of the Duluth Boat Club shows a variety of watercraft, including a man floating in a washtub. The photo also gives some idea of the congestion at the site created by marine traffic. The Duluth Boat Club later moved operations to Park Point to avoid commercial shipping.

NEMHC 52386 b32af13

The only activities of the Duluth Boat Club (before 1900) that were chronicled by the newspapers were the rowing regattas and the annual ball of the club. We may well wonder how the club was generally used by most of its members.

As in most athletic clubs, members used the Duluth Boat Club for exercise, most likely moderate and not intense enough for competition. Members could have paddled their boats around the harbor for a while in the morning or evening, either alone or with friends. Members probably made use of the billiard and reading rooms in the clubhouse, and they may have used the club for entertaining guests. The large room on the third floor was available for private parties, dances, or banquets, and it was almost certainly used in this manner. The club had a number of boats that were

Sailing was one of the important water sports at the Duluth Boat Club. This beautiful trophy for competitive sailing was awarded in 1898 and is from the Saint Louis County Historical Society collection.

Photo by Bruce Ojard Photographics

CHAPTER 1: THE EARLY YEARS 1886–1900

suitable for family outings, and they were doubtless well used for this purpose. Most clubs serve as places to meet friends and make new acquaintances, and this was very likely true of the Duluth Boat Club.

Improbable as it may seem, this club of prestigious and affluent members had its financial problems at times. The club's dues and initiation fees were not always sufficient to cover all of the expenditures. In 1896, the club was $2,400 in debt, but a membership drive brought the club up to two hundred members and $150 in the black by 1898.[22] The boat club was again set back shortly after this when the United States declared war on Spain. Those young men of Duluth who would have been rowers or sailors went off to fight the Spaniards. The club was left deplete of members and money and was, in essence, inactive. The Duluth Boat Club would be financially resurrected again in 1900, but this was a significant turning point in the fortunes of the club and signified the beginning of a new era.

The Duluth Boat Club football team from 1895. It is difficult to say how many other non-boating activities the DBC supported during these early years. NEMHC S2386 "O" box 56

1. Walter Van Brunt, *Duluth and St. Louis County* (New York and Chicago, the American Historical Society, 1921), vol. I, p 67.

2. Ibid.

3. Ibid., vol. I, p. 188.

4. Ibid., vol. I, p. 259.

5. Ibid.

6. Interview with Henning E. Peterson, September 6, 1971.

7. *Articles of Incorporation, Rules, Regulations and By-Laws of the Duluth Boat Club, 1887*, p. 1.

8. Ibid.

9. *Duluth Daily News*, July 14, 1887, p. 8.

10. Ibid.

11. Ibid.

12. Ibid.

13. Ibid.

14. Ibid.

15. (Karl Twedt), Program of the Northwestern International Rowing Association, Saint Paul, MN, July 1970.

16. http://www.hcs.harvard.edu/~harvcrew/Website/History/HY/.

17. *Duluth News Tribune*, July 31, 1894, p.1.

18. *Duluth News Tribune*, July 28, 1895, p.1.

19. Bureau of the Census, Dept. of Commerce, Washington, D.C.

20. *Duluth Daily Tribune*, July 14, 1890, p. 5.

21. *Duluth Daily Tribune*, July 26, 1890, p. 1.

22. Dora Mary MacDonald, *This is Duluth* (Duluth Central High School Printing Dept., 1950), pp. 143-144.

*NEMHC refers to the Northeast Minnesota Historical Center, archives of the St. Louis County Historical Society.

CHAPTER 2

the glory years
1900–1926

Among the oarsmen who were rowing under the auspices of the Duluth Boat Club during the 1890s was Julius Howland Barnes. Barnes was bowman in a crew that won the championship junior four race of the Minnesota-Winnipeg Rowing Association in 1895. Barnes's devotion to the boat club was strong and unwavering. After 1900, his financial and leadership contributions made him the single most important figure in the history of the Duluth Boat Club.

After the boat club had almost ceased to exist during the Spanish-American War in 1898, Barnes led a membership drive in 1900 that made the club stronger than ever.[1] Along with this rejuvenation came a change in the character of the organization. After 1900, the Duluth Boat Club greatly increased the recreational opportunities available to members while continuing to develop athletic activities. The boat club also became less of a men's club and more of a family-oriented organization. As the club expanded and changed, it necessarily lost a degree of its exclusiveness.

Recreational boating was inhibited by the location of the clubhouse, which was situated in the midst of commercial piers. Expansion of the club's facilities was impossible, and increased mercantile water traffic in this area made aquatic recreation hazardous. The second factor that helped change the complexion of the boat club was the building of a new clubhouse on a different site in 1903. The new site on Park Point was only a short distance from the location of the old clubhouse (which was sold), but it was out of the shipping lanes, and the nonindustrial nature of the surrounding land gave ample room for future expansion.

This photo shows the narrow strip of land known as Minnesota Point or "Park Point," which separates Lake Superior from St. Louis Bay and forms the Duluth-Superior Harbor. Nine miles long, Minnesota Point is the largest freshwater sandbar in the world.[2]

Postcard image provided by Jerry Paulson, http://www.duluth-mn-usa.com/

In 1930, Julius Barnes was on the cover of Time magazine as president of the United States Chamber of Commerce. People were looking for a way out of the great economic depression that had settled on the country, and the cover story carried his opinions and outlook.

JULIUS BARNES

The story of Julius Barnes is a rags-to-riches story. When Barnes was thirteen years old, his father died, and he was forced to quit school and find employment as an office boy in a Duluth grain office to help support his family. Six years later, Barnes had his own business as a grain dealer and was soon enormously successful. By the time the First World War began, Barnes was the greatest exporter of wheat in the United States. As chairman of the Erie and Saint Lawrence Corporation at New York, Barnes operated a fleet of freighters along the Great Lakes-Erie Canal and the Atlantic Coast.

When America entered World War I, Barnes became president of the U.S. Grain Corporation under Herbert Hoover's Food Administration. To avoid any suspicion of private gain from war service, he closed all his grain offices and gave his vessel stocks to the YMCA in Duluth. He received no salary for his three years of service. Barnes performed his wartime duties with extreme efficiency, and as a result, he was recognized with service decorations from Britain, France, Italy, Belgium, Poland, Finland, and Bulgaria. This grade school dropout received honorary degrees from Harvard, Dartmouth, Pittsburgh, Syracuse, and William and Mary. Three times Barnes was elected president of the United States Chamber of Commerce and later, three times its chairman. Barnes developed a process for utilizing the previously useless straw from grain in the manufacture of rugs and, consequently, built and operated a rug factory in Duluth. Barnes also owned a shipbuilding facility in Duluth.[1]

JULIUS BARNES (CONTINUED)

Aside from his business, Julius Barnes had two major passions: the city of Duluth and athletics, of which rowing was by far his favorite. Barnes was always endeavoring to boost the fortunes of his native city, and his personal letters show this concern to be sincere. When Barnes was forced to move to New York to run his grain exporting business, he continued to take an interest in Duluth and returned frequently. He was, in fact, known in the business world as "Mr. Barnes of Duluth."

Barnes was convinced that the values instilled in him as a young oarsman formed the foundation of his business success. Rowing does require devotion, sacrifice, and perseverance, and for this reason, Barnes felt that his boat club experience shaped his future. He viewed it as an organization that could help other young men of Duluth become both moral and successful. Barnes often voiced the boat club's ideals, and he once stated:

> The boat club has been a distinct help in the life of this city, . . . the men who have managed it have always had wholesome and healthy ideals and the club and its activities have proven to be a training ground which has developed the capacity for responsibility and organization of many of our young and successful business men . . . The club has always aimed to give the young people of Duluth a place for amusement, to which young people are entitled, and besides that, has a broader ideal of being a great democratic organization which by being the most successful in its own line has typified the best ambitions of this most ambitious city . . . the young men interested in rowing have been taught to get the most out of their skill and ability, and to develop the qualities of endurance and resolution, which I think we all want in our boys.[2]

When Barnes became wealthy, he started endowing the boat club with a generous share of his money. More importantly, perhaps, Barnes took over the club leadership and revamped and guided it according to his own ideals and goals.

The Great Depression came early to the grain trade because of a market glut in grain following World War I. Julius Barnes lost much of his fortune at this time but still remained an important business person for several more decades. These reduced circumstances undoubtedly influenced his withdrawal of financial support for the Duluth Boat Club and the rowing program. After World War II, the Barnes shipbuilding business closed and so did the Klearflax rug factory. In a sad ending to a rich and interesting life, Barnes suffered some very severe business losses in the early 1950s and lived in much reduced circumstances before his death in 1959 at the age of eighty-six.[3]

---

1. Biographical outline from the Julius H. Barnes Collection, NEMHC S3025.

2. Letter to members of the Duluth Boat Club from Julius H. Barnes, president of the Duluth Boat Club, April 25, 1916, from the Duluth Boat Club files, NEMHC S3009.

3. Biographical outline from the Julius H. Barnes Collection, NEMHC S3025.

CHAPTER 2: THE GLORY YEARS 1900–1926

This photo shows just the main clubhouse of the Duluth Boat Club, before the café, tennis courts, and numerous other facilities were built. This is probably the way the DBC clubhouse looked when it opened in 1903. The new clubhouse was larger than the old and included space for rowing shells and other boats, quarters for oarsmen, a clubroom, and a dance floor.

Minnesota Historical Society, Photographer: Charles P. Gibson, Photograph Collection ca. 1900, Location no. MS2.9 DU5.3 p14, Negative no. 5002-A

A crew in a lapstrake four practicing on St. Louis Bay in front of the new DBC clubhouse on Park Point.

Postcard image provided by Jerry Paulson, http://www.duluth-mn-usa.com/

The opening of the new clubhouse in 1903 was similar to the celebration opening the old building in 1887. The newspaper's society columnist stated, "The event was one of the most notable that has occurred in Duluth social circles for months, and many of the 500 who danced away the evening are habitués of the most exclusive ballrooms of the city."[3]

The selling of life memberships for $100 each financed the new facilities, along with eleven new rowboats and three new canoes. In 1903, the club had 250 members, which was a full quota for that period. Applicants had to be placed on waiting lists to prevent crowding.[4]

It wasn't long before the DBC expanded the facility to include a café where members could eat lunch or supper. A table d'hôte luncheon cost thirty-five cents and supper, fifty cents, even when entrees included items such as prime rib of beef, lamb, or lake trout. If the offering for a particular day seemed unsatisfactory to a diner, he could order something else from a menu, such as a sirloin steak for sixty cents.[5]

25

INVINCIBLE: HISTORY OF THE DULUTH BOAT CLUB

The main boathouse of the Duluth Boat Club is on the right with the club restaurant located on the left. There is a walkway connecting these buildings that goes over a waterway between other boat storage buildings, which cannot be seen in this photo.
NEMHC 52422 b5f1

The interior of the Duluth Boat Club Café, which had windows on all four sides, offered an exciting view of harbor activity, the downtown area, and the Duluth hills in the background.

Under Barnes's leadership, the boat club continued to expand. In 1906, a branch of the club was established at Oatka Beach on Park Point, three miles south of the main clubhouse. Located here were dressing rooms for bathers, an open pavilion for picnic parties, and facilities for boats. A matron was employed to assist ladies and children, to make coffee, and to furnish dishes and silverware for picnickers. By 1906, the club had acquired a large fleet of pleasure boats, and many of these were kept at Oatka.

The addition of the Oatka Branch improved the boat club considerably. Previously, someone wishing to paddle a boat or canoe three miles needed to stay within a mile and a half of the main house. With the new branch, one could paddle the three miles to Oatka, leave the boat there, and take the streetcar back to the main house. The streetcar running on Minnesota Point made the Oatka Branch very accessible.

The area surrounding the Oatka Branch was more rustic than the neighborhood around the main house. The north end of Minnesota Point, where the main house was located, was residential, while the Oatka Branch was set in a pine forest that did not have much development except for the streetcar track. It was a beautiful place for swimming, if one could tolerate the usually frigid water of Lake Superior or the somewhat murky water of the harbor, which was beginning to show signs of the pollution that would increase with the years to come.

In addition to the café, the Duluth Boat Club also developed two tennis courts, which were built on fill brought in for that purpose. Tennis became an important and popular program at the DBC. The tennis courts in this photo are in the foreground of another new building, which had additional covered slips for boats.

NEMHC 52422 b5f1

This picture postcard shows the Oatka Branch of the Duluth Boat Club in its beautiful setting on St. Louis Bay, only a few yards from the beach on Lake Superior.

Postcard image provided by Jerry Paulson, http://www.duluth-mn-usa.com/

This picture postcard shows the pine forest of Park Point penetrated only by the streetcar tracks that ran from the aerial bridge past both the main clubhouse and the Oatka branch of the Duluth Boat Club.

Postcard image provided by Jerry Paulson, http://www.duluth-mn-usa.com/

The new boathouse of the Duluth Boat Club was an impressive landmark for the city and was featured on picture postcards for years. Here is a sample.

Postcard image provided by Jerry Paulson, http://www.duluth-mn-usa.com/

INVINCIBLE: HISTORY OF THE DULUTH BOAT CLUB

The clay tennis courts at the Oatka Branch were among the finest in Minnesota and were set in a pine forest only yards away from the Lake Superior beach.

Copy of original photograph (photographer unknown) provided by Chip Jacobs.

Within a few years of the opening of the Oatka Branch, the Duluth Boat Club built four clay tennis courts at this site. The construction of these tennis courts out of clay required special engineering, because the sand, of which Minnesota Point is entirely composed, absorbed moisture, drying out the clay and making it crack. It was necessary to lay down a heavy foundation of red clay to retain the water and make a solid foundation. This was then surfaced with a fine clay dredged from the bottom of the St. Louis River. As a result, these were the finest tennis courts in Minnesota and neighboring states.[6] Consequently, the Duluth Boat Club annually hosted the tournament for the Minnesota state tennis championship on these courts for many years. Tennis became one of the main activities sponsored by the boat club.

In 1907, the Duluth Boat Club made even further expansion. Property was purchased on the St. Louis River at Spirit Lake, twelve miles upstream from the main house. Although the Spirit Lake Branch was located within the city limits of Duluth, it was in an uninhabited area. There was no sign of the industry or population of the city. On this part of the river, there were only trees, water, hills, and wildlife.

At Spirit Lake, the boat club built a number of pretty cottages and a dormitory on a bluff overlooking the river, and they placed picnic tables under a shady grove. Built over the water were a boathouse, a dining room, and a dance floor. The front veranda overlooked the river for miles.[7] The boat club soon built two clay tennis courts at the Spirit Lake Branch.

The Spirit Lake Branch provided a splendid location for nature lovers. This part of the river has many bays, inlets, tributaries, and islands that invite exploration. Especially suited for exploring canoeists was the Red River, which flows into the St. Louis several miles upstream from Spirit Lake. The Red River has miles of meandering backwater, with tree

CHAPTER 2: THE GLORY YEARS 1900–1926

The Oatka Branch gave the Duluth Boat Club a wonderful location for family picnics and a destination for canoe paddlers. Oatka was three miles southeast of the main boathouse and was located on the streetcar line. This photo shows the amazing amount of activity taking place at Oatka during the summer. There were also four clay tennis courts at Oatka that are not shown in this photo.
Photo from 1911 Mid-Summer Water Carnival—Duluth 1911 Souvenir Program. From the author's collection

branches nearly meeting overhead, forming a bower over the stream. In 1907, the St. Louis River, the Spirit Lake area, and upstream were still unpolluted, and the fishing was excellent.

Previously, the Duluth Boat Club ceased its activities during the winter, but the Spirit Lake Branch was open all year. Duck hunting was a popular activity there in the fall. In the winter, the Spirit Lake Branch offered snowshoeing, skiing, skating, or improvised hockey on the river ice and sleigh rides. After these vigorous pastimes, the members welcomed the prospect of supper before a blazing fire in the club dining room.[8]

The Spirit Lake Branch of the DBC was located on the St. Louis River about twelve miles upstream from the main boathouse in the community that later became Morgan Park. There were cottages for overnight stays and buildings for picnics. Boats and canoes were available for paddling trips in the quiet and beautiful St. Louis River estuary. The Spirit Lake Branch had a train station on the property, and members could catch a train to travel to and from downtown Duluth.

29

INVINCIBLE: HISTORY OF THE DULUTH BOAT CLUB

The Spirit Lake Branch was kept open during the winter and was the place for skating parties, bonfires, and winter picnics.
NEMHC 52386 b32af13

Launch was the most enjoyable means of reaching Spirit Lake, the trip being a pleasure in itself. The boat club owned several motor launches, ranging from a small fast launch carrying four to six passengers to a large cabin launch carrying thirty-five people. Members could rent any size launch for two dollars per hour, which included the services of a club employee who drove the boat. Those who were not inclined to make the trip by water could reach the Spirit Lake Branch by train. A railroad line cut across a corner of the boat club property and the club had a private station on its grounds.[9]

The Duluth Boat Club expanded dramatically between 1904 and 1907, both in terms of increased membership and the size of the physical plant. The membership increased from 195 to 700 members, and the harbor frontage owned increased from 120 feet to 586 feet while gross income and property value increased by approximately 500 percent. The Duluth Boat Club began to make the claim that it was the best, as well as the largest, water club in America. This claim does not seem to have been disputed.[10]

To show the new members how the boat club's extensive facilities could be used, Julius Barnes wrote a hypothetical diary of a club member, which was printed in a memorandum and mailed to all members. This hypothetical diary shows us a glimpse of the boat club in operation and also provides some insight as to how Barnes personally perceived the Duluth Boat Club and its relation to Duluth.[11]

Monday

"Weather being pleasant, I took a most attractive lady and went down to the main house of the Duluth Boat Club. Now, this was just a short walk—only 3 blocks in fact, below the aerial bridge. We had supper in the café at a large window overlooking the harbor and it was certainly a beautiful outlook just out of the path of the big freighters. Our meal was the regular table d'hôte supper of the club, 50 cents, and was well served. After supper, we took a canoe, paddling down along the shore enjoying the panorama of cottages, trees and summer camps. We left our canoe at the Oatka Branch of the club just above the White City and after strolling about the White City, came home on an open car—a most delightful ride."

Tuesday

"Left the office early today and took the car for Oatka. At the Oatka Branch, I rented a bathing suit of the boatman and had an enjoyable swim. Found the bottom was clean and sandy and deepened so gradually I did not wonder at finding a number of women and children also enjoying the bathing at the point. After dressing, I took a rowboat, and the 3-mile row up to the main house of the club gave me a most vigorous appetite for supper. The evening meal was good, as before, and I spent the evening on the veranda smoking and watching the parties in and out of the house. I was surprised to find so many people, young and old, using the house on such a pleasant evening. Both the pleasure boats and the launches were busy a large part of the evening. The row or paddle between Oatka and the main house seems to be just about right for most people and I found a large number of parties taking the boat at one place and returning it at the other."

Wednesday

"I had heard so much about the new Spirit Lake Branch of the Duluth Boat Club that I was curious to see it. I telephoned the boatman at the main house in the morning and was surprised to learn that he could furnish a launch of any capacity, from a fast launch carrying 4 to 6 passengers to a large cabin launch carrying 30 to 35 people. The charge for this was $2 per hour for a launch of any size driven by an experience engineer . . . I made up a party of four and took the fast "D.B.C." up to Spirit Lake. It is as pretty as has been pictured. The cottages are picturesquely situated on a bluff heavily wooded, overlooking the river, and with an outlook up and down the river, which is unrivalled. I find they have cottages there and sleeping accommodations for families and for young

The Bobwhite was one of several motor launches owned by the Duluth Boat Club and could be used for a trip up river to the Spirit Lake Branch.

people. . . The supper we had was their regular table d'hôte supper served at 40 cents, and everything we had was delicious. I found the buildings, the grounds, and the dock lighted by a new acetylene gas plant, which has just been put in by the Carbolite Works. It works perfectly and the grounds are beautifully lighted in this manner at night. We watched the Newsboy stop at the dock on its way back to the city, taking home the same people who had come up on the Newsboy earlier in the day. We found a number of people arriving at six o'clock, having left the Union Depot on the train leaving there at 5:30 and stopping at the boat club's platform on its grounds at Spirit Lake. It is certainly a most convenient place to reach after all, and now that it has its new telephone connections, it will be easy to plan ahead for parties to be catered for here. . . . The matron tells me that she had had as many

as fifty people at supper on one evening and cared for them all satisfactorily. The run down the river just about dark was beautiful, and we found it took just an hour and twenty minutes between the Spirit Lake Branch and the main boathouse."

Thursday

"Some of the young people wanted a basket picnic down on Park Point today, and I fell in with their plans at once. The only amendment I suggested was, instead of going over on the sand where things are inconvenient and you get somewhat cramped trying to eat like a Turk or a shoemaker, that we go up to the Oatka Branch and we use their picnic tables on the open pavilion upstairs. We did this and had the matron at the branch make our coffee. She furnished cream and sugar and we also got dishes of her. We found her most obliging and on the upper promenade sheltered from the northeast wind, and with the outlook over the bay, we enjoyed our supper most thoroughly. The matron tells me that on a pleasant evening this summer they have had as many as 80 or 100 picnickers there with their supper. After supper, we took the canoes and rowboats from the Oatka house and floated down the bay just off the White City, watching the lights and listening to the music. Then we took the car home."

Friday

"I had some out-of-town visitors come in on me unexpectedly today and made up a party for their amusement. We decided to go up the river to the Spirit Lake Branch again and I telephoned the boatman at the boat club to have a launch carrying 30 people for me at half past three. We went to the club at that hour and it was ready, and

Detail from a famous panorama of the Duluth Boat Club taken in 1909. Notice the tremendous variety and amount of activity in this photo.

Photo from the Lake Superior Maritime Collections at the Jim Dan Hill Library at the University of Wisconsin, Superior. This is a detail copy from the original panoramic photo at the NEMHC.

we started for Spirit Lake. My out-of-town visitors were certainly enthusiastic about the ride, and it really is hard to find any city that can spread such a panorama of business and commercial activity as our harbor front shows and back it up with the romantic and beautiful scenery that our hills show behind it. I sometimes think that we here in Duluth fail sometimes to appreciate how much this impresses the out-of-town visitors. I telephoned ahead to the Spirit Lake Branch to have supper ready for us by 5:30, and they were all prepared for us when we arrived there. We found several of the launch parties there—some who were on their way back to the city to have some ice cream and coffee or light refreshments. They all seemed to be cared for and to enjoy this feature of the club immensely. We came home down the river by moonlight, and the trip back was even prettier than the one up in the afternoon."

Saturday

"I found there were some afternoon water sports on at the main house of the club and went down early to enjoy them. . . There were boat races, log birling, swimming, diving, and a game of water baseball that was very amusing to those who had never seen it. There was a large crowd to supper but the steward has systemized the dining room so that they are handled with comparatively little friction—not more than you would find in any summer resort on a pleasant day crowded for a meal. . . There was quite a party of us and we stayed for supper. We then took the boat out for an hour on the bay and came back in time for dancing in the evening. These

Saturday night 'hops' at the boat club seem to be very popular. The floor is undoubtedly the best dancing floor in the Northwest, at least that I have seen around Duluth, and the music is perfect. Everybody who likes to dance seems to have a good time—both young and old. There are a lot of older members who simply enjoy sitting on the veranda, watching the young people and listening to the music. Certainly there are very few cities that can show a panorama of lights and shadows at night like Duluth and very few clubs that are fortunate enough to have such an outlook as the Duluth Boat Club has from its upper veranda. Parties were coming and going all evening. The café was open all evening and we had a delicious dish of ice cream and hot coffee. . . Duluth's position on the waterfront is unique, and it should be used for the enjoyment of Duluth residents and their visitors. The Duluth Boat Club seems to be fully alive to this and certainly has kept apace with the growth of the city in devising and extending its facilities for enjoyment."

This "diary" leaves the impression that the Duluth Boat Club was a very wholesome organization. The club was indeed wholesome, which directly reflected the values and leadership of Julius Barnes. Barnes's personal letters show that he was steadfastly against the use of alcohol. In fact, he would write letters to national magazines in his later years, urging them not only to refrain from liquor advertisements, but also to refrain from using pictures of businessmen's clubs that showed businessmen drinking alcoholic beverages, since he thought that such illustrations presented a distorted image. It is not surprising that there is no record of liquor ever being served or consumed at the boat club.

The boat club encouraged activities for young men and women, but set limits. The official boat club policy on matters sexual can be inferred from a notice concerning club dances that was published in the Duluth Boat Club Log of 1920.

Dancers Please Note!
We regret that it should again be necessary to call attention of a few of our members to the rules against "Cheek to Cheek" dancing . . . The club is no place for the "Cheek to Cheek," the "Shimmy" or other of the late vulgar forms of modern dancing . . . The club has always had the reputation of giving the best dances in the city—the type of dances mothers will allow their daughters to attend without the least hesitation. We are proud of that reputation and WE ARE GOING TO CONTINUE TO GIVE THAT SORT OF DANCES.

Dancing constituted as large a part of boat club activities as boating. In 1909, the Duluth Boat Club took over the defunct Duluth Yacht Club. During the winter, the old Yacht Club building was slid down the ice of the harbor to Oatka, providing that branch with both a restaurant and dance hall.[12] From that time on, dances were held nightly at Oatka, which was supposed to have had the finest dance floor in the city.[13] The nightly dances at Oatka were open to the general public for an admission charge. Dances were

The Venetian Fete was a nighttime display of watercraft ornamented with lights and papier-mâché decorating the Duluth Harbor around the festive main facility of the Duluth Boat Club, which was also festooned with lights and decorations. This nighttime extravaganza was a very popular part of the annual DBC Water Carnival, as can be seen by the throngs of people in this photo.

NEMHC 52422 b5f4

CHAPTER 2: THE GLORY YEARS 1900–1926

also held at the main house on weekends, and dances were held at Spirit Lake whenever anyone felt inclined to organize one. The club also permitted members to use its three ballrooms for private parties under certain regulations, schedule permitting.[14] The Duluth Boat Club hired a dance instructor to tutor interested members in gymnastic, folk, and modern dancing.[15]

The piece written by Barnes gives an almost complete idea of what the boat club had to offer in 1907, but there were many additions to Duluth Boat Club activities after it was written that are worthy of mention. In 1907, the Duluth Boat Club held its first "Venetian Fete," which was to become an annual event for many years. Patterned after the water carnivals of old Venice, the Venetian Fete was a gaudy visual spectacle of decorated watercraft. The Fete was held at night. More than a hundred launches, rowboats, and canoes were lavishly trimmed with lighted Japanese lanterns. The vessels formed a water parade, led by an orchestra seated on a gaily decorated flatboat towed by a launch. Colored searchlights from the boat club's main house played across the water. Prizes were given for the best decorated boat, so participants strove to outdo each other in the decorating. In 1907, ten thousand spectators viewed this brilliant spectacle of color, light, and music.[16] The size and popularity of the Venetian Fete grew even greater in subsequent years.

In 1911, the Venetian Fete was described by the *Duluth News Tribune*, which reported, "Nearly 200 gorgeously bedecked, ornamented, and artistically draped canoes glided through a blazing sea of reflected light, a perfect blending of light and color." The boats were often decorated to resemble animals. Dragons seemed especially popular, as someone attempted to decorate his boat this way nearly every year. In 1911, the prize-winning canoe was

INVINCIBLE: HISTORY OF THE DULUTH BOAT CLUB

One of the "floats" for the Venetian Fete decorated as a dragon. In the 1911 Venetian Fete, there were almost two hundred of these floats.

decorated as a butterfly. It had huge mechanically operated yellow wings and electric decorated eyes.[17] The materials for decorating the boats (lanterns, tissue paper, and wood lattice) were provided for members by the boat club free of charge.[18] By 1911, there were four double tennis courts at the main house, and for the Venetian Fete, these courts were also lit by the light of Japanese lanterns. There was dancing upon these courts all night and in the main hall as well.[19]

Not only did the Venetian Fete grow larger after 1907, it became just part of a large water carnival that spanned several days. The water carnivals were usually planned around rowing regattas, which were the feature event. In 1911, the Duluth Boat Club hosted the annual regatta of the North-Western International Rowing Association, which spread its races out over a two-day period. In addition to the rowing contests and the Venetian Fete, the 1911 water carnival included sailing races, motorboat races, canoe races (including women's war canoe races—sixteen women per canoe), swimming races, diving exhibitions, water baseball, log birling, canoe tilting, canoe wrestling, water pushball, duck chasing by swimmers, drill and exhibition of the U.S. Coast Guard lifesaving crew and cutter, and whaleboat races by the U.S. Naval Reserves.[20]

The largest spectacle in the 1911 water carnival was a staging of the famous naval duel between the ironclads *Monitor* and *Merrimac* at Hampton Roads, Virginia, in 1862. Boats were arranged to resemble the ironclads and the various frigates, and these vessels were given commanders. The sham battle began with an exchange of shots, and soon the frigates were burning or sinking, as they had been filled with combustible material and well saturated with oil.

Women's war canoe racing was a popular activity and an important event at the annual club water carnival. NEMHC 52422 b5f3

Log rolling or birling was another source of competition and amusement at the Duluth Water Carnival.
NEMHC 52422 b5f3

Water baseball was one of the events at the annual Duluth Water Carnival held by the DBC.
NEMHC 52422 b5f3

A lot of the fun at the Duluth Boat Club was unorganized and spontaneous.

The cover of the program from the 1911 Duluth Mid-Summer Water Carnival.

From the personal collection of the author

INVINCIBLE: HISTORY OF THE DULUTH BOAT CLUB

The boats representing the ironclads, frigates, and revenue cutters were faithful reproductions of the original vessels. As planned, most of the crafts were utterly destroyed in the mock battle, which was apparently quite a sight.[21]

The boat club financed these water carnivals, at least in part, by building a grandstand and charging spectators for admission (two dollars per seat for the duration of the entire carnival in 1911).

The water carnival was held annually. Subsequent water carnivals differed from the 1911 water carnival in some particulars, but they were basically similar. The annual water carnival was not only the largest affair that the boat club sponsored for the benefit of the public, it was the biggest event of the year for the city of Duluth. The water carnival served not only as entertainment, but also as public relations on the city's behalf. This feeling was expressed by the *Duluth News Tribune*: "As a civic celebration and advertiser of Duluth, the carnival was as much of a success as it was in the amusement line."[22]

There were other festivities sponsored by the boat club. The "Lawn Fete" at Spirit Lake is an example. An outdoor band concert started the evening, after which refreshments were served and music and dancing was begun. The grounds were lit up with hundreds of lights for the occasion. To assure that all members who wished to attend the Lawn Fete had adequate transportation, special trains and streetcars were scheduled during the evening. This was not a public affair, but the size of the Duluth Boat Club's membership made the gathering quite large. About eight hundred people attended.[23]

Trophies that were awarded at the Duluth Mid-Summer Water Carnival.

NEMHC 52422 B5f2

Besides the extravaganzas, there were many smaller happenings put on by the boat club. Every Tuesday evening, there was an informal party at the Oatka Branch. During good weather, these Tuesday evening get-togethers would often begin with

Boys dive off the DBC high dive located off the corner of the tennis courts.

NEMHC 52422 b5f3

CHAPTER 2: THE GLORY YEARS 1900–1926

some impromptu water sports. Then the gathering would sing songs for a while and finish the evening dancing to an orchestra.[24] Also popular were the frequent barn and Spanish dances held on the moonlit tennis courts at the main house.

Besides the Duluth Water Carnival, several other annual events were held at the boat club. Every year, the Duluth Boat Club had a Ladies Day, where the ladies were given the opportunity to demonstrate their athletic prowess. Tennis matches, sailboat races, motorboat races, and rowing races were held, all for ladies only.[25] Ladies Day put an emphasis on the fact that the Duluth Boat Club made an effort to provide as many aquatic recreation programs for females as they did for males.

The handwritten caption on the back of this photograph from the 1911 Duluth Water Carnival program says "Ladies Day at the Boat Club." On Ladies Day, all activities were for women, and, therefore, we are left to assume that this large flotilla of sailboats, the two war canoes, and the two rowing eights at the dock were all crewed by women.

Another annual event that provided members with much amusement was a baseball game where the bachelors would challenge the married men.[26] The boat club held a College Day, which honored all of Duluth's college men that graduated that year. College Day served to publicize the intellectual endeavors of Duluth's young citizens, and it provided an opportunity to persuade these scholars to remain in Duluth and consider joining the Duluth Boat Club.[27]

Sailboats cross the finish line in front of the Duluth Boat Club grandstand.   NEMHC 52422 b5f3

Sailing was an important Boat Club program. Since the switch in location of the Duluth Boat Club in 1903, the club was able to offer facilities for the mooring of sailboats owned by members. The club provided a protected anchorage for sailboats, a marine railway for hauling boats out of the water for either storage or repair, a large shed for winter storage, floats, pumps, dinghies, and sailors' quarters.[28] The conveniences for boat owners were complete by 1910, as a memo from March 26 of that year stated, "The club will, when requested, make all ordinary repairs to privately owned boats and engines at the Main House and the 14th Street shop, employing only experienced workman, and the club charging for same the cost of the material and a low price for time (45 cents per hour)."

Sailboats race on Lake Superior and St. Louis Bay. NEMHC 52422 b5f3

Quite a few Duluth Boat Club members owned their own sailboats. Here is a photo of Walker Jamar and his wife Clare sailing their twenty-eight-foot sloop Seagull on St. Louis Bay. Jamar and the Seagull were top competitors in the Boat Club's annual sailing series in the A division of the twenty-eight knockabout racing class. In 1915, Jamar won the "Commercial Cup." For several years, Jamar was "captain" of the DBC sailing program and later became club president.

Photo provided from the personal collection of Walker Jamar Jr.

CHAPTER 2: THE GLORY YEARS 1900–1926

Duluth Boat Club pennants. Photo by Bruce Ojard Photographics from the Duluth Boat Club collection of the St. Louis County Historical Society.

The boat club also owned sailboats for the benefit of its members that didn't own one. In 1912, the club had a couple of twenty-two-foot sailboats for rent to members for twenty-five cents per hour.[29] In 1913, the club had two thirty-two-foot sailboats.[30] To ensure that their equipment was less likely to be damaged and their members less likely to drown, the Duluth Boat Club offered sailing lessons to neophyte sailors.[31] For the experienced yachtsmen, the club instituted a seasonal sailing tournament. During the 1913 sailing season, fifty-four men sailed out of the boat club in racing crews every Saturday afternoon.[32]

By keeping an abundance of boats, the boat club sought to ensure that some type of watercraft would always be available to its members. Besides the motor launches, sailboats, and rowing shells (racing variety) in 1913, the club had eighty-one sixteen-foot canoes, nine eighteen-foot canoes, and thirty rowboats.[33] The number of boats on hand fluctuated from year to year, but there were usually about as many as in 1913. In addition, some of the rowing shells were available for the use of noncompetitive members, as well as the club athletes. To keep in shape, Barnes used to scull a few miles every morning before beginning the day's business.[34]

As the automobile came into use and auto excursions to nearby lakes became popular, the Duluth Boat Club established another branch at Pike Lake, several miles north of Duluth. The Pike Lake Branch had canoes and boats, a pavilion, dressing rooms with bathing suits for rent, and a screened porch for picnic

In 1913, the Duluth Boat Club hosted a canoe regatta called "Lark o' the Lake," which was intended to be an annual competition. This drawing from the cover of the program also shows a women's war canoe in the foreground, and in the background is the flying boat owned by the DBC. The flying boat was also named "Lark o' the Lake."

43

INVINCIBLE: HISTORY OF THE DULUTH BOAT CLUB

In 1913, Julius Barnes purchased this flying boat for his own use, but his bankers who financed his worldwide grain trade would not let him fly because it was considered too dangerous. So, Barnes made the flying boat available to the Duluth Boat Club. Tony Janus was the pilot. According to The Zenith, *the Duluth Boat Club owned the flying boat in 1914.*

Photo from The Zenith, *July 1916, from the personal collection of David Bjorkman*

parties.[35] In addition to the major activities of the boat club already mentioned, the Duluth Boat Club provided for camping by renting tents to members for a slight charge. Another activity the Duluth Boat Club offered was water skiing, which may have been more novel than popular. The boat club even sponsored a basketball team during the winter months.

If there was any doubt that the Duluth Boat Club was the best as well as largest water club in America in 1907, there was no uncertainty by 1913. By this time, the Duluth Boat Club had all the facilities and activities that have been mentioned, and the club's rowing crews had started to establish their national dominance, which would continue for a decade. The membership had grown to 1,400 by 1910 and remained at this number in 1913.[36]

This is the only known photo of the Pike Lake Branch of the Duluth Boat Club. Unfortunately, not much of the facility is in view in this photo.

NEMHC 52386 b32af13

The boat club must have grown less exclusive in order for it to grow to 1,400 members. There is no record that the complex membership procedure called for by the *Articles of Incorporation, Rules, Regulations and By-Laws of 1886* was officially changed or dispensed with, but it seems likely that people could belong to the club if they could afford it. The membership drives oftentimes netted several hundred additional members within days.

The cost of belonging to the club did change. In 1911, the initiation fee was thirty dollars, and the annual dues were twenty dollars. Memberships were for individuals, but ladies escorted by gentlemen members of the club needed no membership card. Children under twelve could use the club facilities when accompanied by a parent or guardian who was a club member. Children of club members who were between the ages of thirteen and twenty-one were issued junior cards, which cost five dollars apiece.[37] It is estimated that since each membership provided access to the club for the entire family of the member, probably more than five thousand individuals were using the club through these memberships.

Despite the array of recreation offered by the Duluth Boat Club, the club experienced a downward turn after 1913. The membership declined to eight hundred members in 1915.[38] The club leadership, Julius Barnes in particular, expressed concern and puzzlement over the waning interest in the Duluth Boat Club. They had made their club the largest and best water club in America, and now they found, to their surprise and frustration, that people were ceasing to care about the boat club. Barnes stated his feeling in an open letter to club members:[39]

> *Owing to various causes, perhaps among others the replacement by the automobile of the motor-boats, the club membership has declined until it is no longer self-sustaining, even though the club has always been relieved of the direct expenses of rowing entirely. Is there not local pride enough in the organization to maintain a membership list in this city of 100,000 that can keep the club paying its way? Does it not furnish enough amusement and entertainment for people of all ages to justify its scale of dues?*

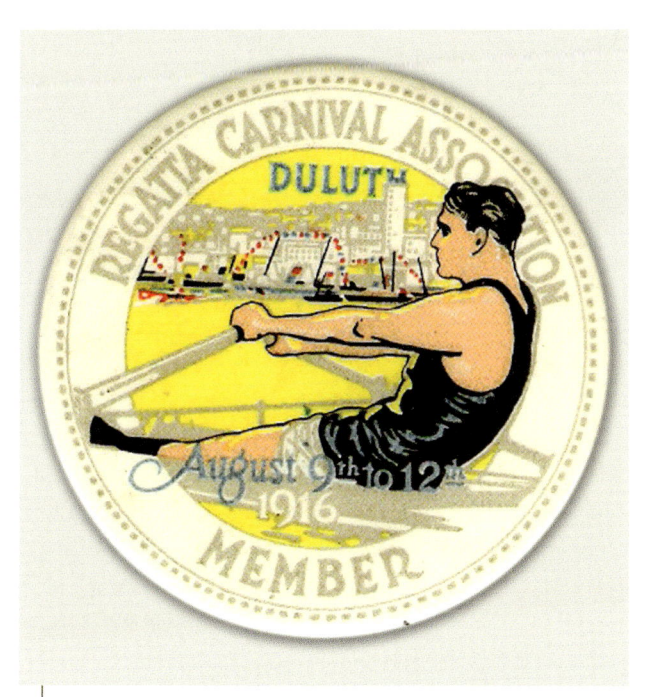

To promote and help fund the 1916 Regatta and Carnival, the Duluth Boat Club sold promotional buttons, such as the one shown here.

From the personal collection of the author

In 1915, the Spirit Lake Branch of the club was closed, but this closing was not due to retrenchment. The newly organized U.S. Steel Corporation opened a steel plant on Spirit Lake in the immediate vicinity of the boat club property in 1915. The beautiful natural ambience of the upper part of the St. Louis River estuary transitioned to heavy industry. The Pike Lake Branch of the club dropped out of mention in the Duluth Boat Club correspondence, and there began to be occasional references in the newspapers to the Auto Club's Pike Lake property. Henning E. Peterson confirmed that the Auto Club property was formerly the Duluth Boat Club's Pike Lake Branch.[40]

While the club was experiencing a setback in membership and facilities, the rowing crews were getting stronger. In the 1915 national regatta, the Duluth oarsmen were so completely victorious that Julius Barnes was able to persuade the National Association of Amateur Oarsmen to hold their annual championship regatta in Duluth in 1916. Naturally, the club officers were eager to bring the Duluth Boat Club back to peak operation for this nationally publicized event. By dropping the initiation fee from thirty dollars to ten dollars and by intensive recruitment, the membership was increased to 1,262.[41]

The enthusiasm of the Duluthians was almost unbounded. The 1916 National Championship Regatta was included in a huge water carnival, which was much like the water carnivals described earlier except that the city went all out because of the national attention brought by the championship regatta. The first day of the water carnival was dedicated to Julius Barnes, in recognition of his efforts to make Duluth famous for water recreation. The carnival officially opened with a water pageant depicting the arrival of King Neptune and his court, who were supposed to rule the city for the duration of the water carnival. People came dressed in costumes as pirates, Indians, gay harlequins, and ruby princesses, among others. After the formal reception of King Neptune, there was a street celebration, in which the newspaper estimated that perhaps as many as fifty thousand people participated.[42] The rest of the 1916 water carnival was much like the previous water carnivals, except that it included the National Regatta as the central event. Typical of the general enthusiasm was a song composed for the water carnival by M. M. Hanna and printed in the *Duluth News Tribune*. It was titled "When Old Duluth Puts On Her Rowin' Togs, Look Out."[43] It not only seemed as though Duluthians were sacrificing sophistication for zeal, this was, in fact, official policy. After the carnival, an editorial stated, "Duluth shed its dignity like a false face and resumed the spirit of youth."[44]

CHAPTER 2: THE GLORY YEARS 1900–1926

In addition to the championship rowing races, the Duluth Boat Club also had rowing races for boys and girls. Two girls' rowing teams trained at the Boat Club all summer to race each other at the 1916 water carnival. This is a photo of the "Red" team that won the event from the "Green" team.

Photo provided by David Rutford. ND Photographer unknown

Challenge cups awarded for the rowing "Junior Division" during the 1916 Water Carnival. The trophy to the left was for the girls eight. The trophy in the center was for the boys eight, and the trophy to the right was for the boys quad.

Photo by Bruce Ojard of artifacts from the Duluth Boat Club collection of the St. Louis County Historical Society

In addition to the elaborate water carnival events, the club officers prepared for the National Regatta of 1916 by investing more money in facilities. A new building for rowing shells was built for $7,592 and a dormitory for oarsmen for $2,000. The club spent $4,424 for furniture and fixtures and $1,400 for new rowboats and canoes. A new grandstand was built, one-eighth of a mile long, at a cost of $7,500. Since the club charged admission to the grandstand, some expenses were defrayed by the National Regatta, which made $10,700 for the club. Still, after everything was balanced out, the Duluth Boat Club stood $28,000 in debt at the end of the 1916 season.[45]

The National Regatta was a huge success, and it gained the favorable attention of the national press. Perhaps Barnes was made optimistic by the apparent comeback that the boat club made in 1916 because he decided to donate a natatorium to the club. A natatorium is a structurally separate building containing a swimming pool. The natatorium was built next to the main house and was opened on the fourth of July in 1917. This natatorium cost Barnes $75,000 and was the finest swimming facility in Minnesota—the largest and most modern. The tiled swimming pool measured thirty-five by seventy-five feet and had heated water, which was filtered and sterilized. There was also a small pool for children and beginners. The pool was enclosed in a large heated building with dressing rooms and showers, and overhead skylights provided natural lighting.[46]

Barnes made it a club objective that all of its members should know how to swim. To help achieve this goal, he not only donated the natatorium, he also hired the best-known swimming instructor and coach in the country, Mathew Mann. Before coming to Duluth, Mann was swimming coach at Yale University. He later went on to become swim coach at the University of Michigan where he won eight NCAA team championships in a row, twelve in fifteen years, and thirteen overall to stamp him the United States' most successful college coach. He was also head coach of the U.S. Olympic swimming team, and his team won the 1952 Olympic swim events. When he retired from the University of Michigan at age seventy, he went on to coach eight years at Oklahoma, never losing a Big 8 swimming meet.[47]

The natatorium quickly became a chief focal point of the boat club. A gold medal was given to the person who swam the most lengths of the pool (lengths had to be monitored) during the season. The club swimmers were divided into teams, with girls, boys, good swimmers, poor swimmers, etc., evenly distributed. Names such as minnows, whales, pollywogs, and sharks were given the various teams, and every Thursday night the teams would compete against each other.[48]

Nationally famous swimmers came to compete in the new natatorium. Johnny Weissmuller, an Olympic swimming champion who would go on to star in Tarzan movies, won his first major swimming race at the Duluth Boat Club.[49] One evening at the boat club, Duke Kahanamoku broke the world record for 125 yards by two seconds, and Clarence Lane broke the world record for the forty-yard dash by four-fifths of a second.[50]

The Duluth swimmers quickly became nationally competitive. In 1920, Mel Coolly from the Duluth Boat Club won the one-mile national AAU junior swimming championship. At the same swim meet in Detroit, Miss Kulman from Duluth took second place in the national long distance swimming championship for women, and a Duluth Boat Club team took second place in Central AAU relay for women.[51] Ellen Neville also won the women's 220-yard junior freestyle in 1920.[52]

Barnes had hoped that the addition of the natatorium would rejuvenate interest in the Boat Club and keep the membership at least up to the level that the National Regatta of 1916 had brought it. The natatorium did accomplish this objective to a degree, but about the same time that it started operating, the United States entered World War I. Many of the young men who were the target market for the Duluth Boat Club programs left the city to serve in the armed forces.

An exterior view of the natatorium purchased by Julius Barnes for the Duluth Boat Club. It was the finest swimming facility in the state of Minnesota. In 1920, there were two AAU national championship swimming races held at this facility.

NEMHC 52422 b5f1

CHAPTER 2: THE GLORY YEARS 1900–1926

An interior view of the natatorium. NEMHC 53025 B12f4

Two young swimmers in the interior of the natatorium. NEMHC 2386 b32af13

INVINCIBLE: HISTORY OF THE DULUTH BOAT CLUB

The Duluth Boat Club Swim Team from 1922. Duluth Public Library Slide Collection

During the war years, the Duluth Boat Club oriented its programs toward a younger age group. National rowing competition ceased during the war. The Duluth Boat Club did not allow draft-age males to take part in the club's rowing program. However, the rowing program was kept alive with high school–aged boys manning the oars and racing each other.

The DBC started a summer camp for youngsters in 1916, which continued throughout the war years. These camps became one of the Boat Club's major activities. The girls and boys attending these camps used the oarsmen's facilities, including their training table. They were tutored in rowing, swimming, sailing, canoeing, boxing, wrestling, baseball, hiking, and military drills. One of those who participated in the summer camp of 1918 was the son of Herbert Hoover, future president of the United States.[53] Another person who attended these camps was Mrs. Alison (then McBean) Buckingham. In a taped interview (no date) for the Saint Louis County Historical Society, Mrs. Buckingham gave a vivid description of what it was like for a young person to belong to the Duluth Boat Club. She loved the everyday aspects of the club, being able to spend an entire day at the boat club engaging in a variety of recreational activities. Mrs. Buckingham gives a beautiful description of how it was to take a canoe out at dusk and watch the sun set behind the hills and later look up at the light dotting the central hillside. Her description of dancing at night on a dance floor built out over the bay is poetic. Mrs. Buckingham felt that the Duluth Boat Club offered a young person everything that he could possibly want to do. Mrs. Buckingham left Duluth in 1920. When she returned many years later for a visit, she was surprised and sad to find that the Duluth Boat Club no longer existed.

CHAPTER 2: THE GLORY YEARS 1900–1926

1. Dora Mary MacDonald, "This is Duluth" (Duluth Central High School Printing Dept., 1950), p. 144.

2. William G. Loy, "The Evolution of Bay-Head Bars in Western Lake Superior," *Publication No. 10*, Great Lakes Research Division, Univ. of Michigan, 1963.

3. *Duluth News Tribune*, June 28, 1903, p. 1.

4. *Duluth News Tribune*, June 5, 1903, p. 10.

5. Memorandum for DBC members, undated, unclassified, J. D. Mahoney Scrapbook, Duluth Boat Club records, NEMHC S3009

6. *Duluth Herald*, July 12, 1925, p. 10.

7. Duluth Boat Club 1908 (yearbook), NEMHC 52386 b32af13.

8. Ibid.

9. Ibid.

10. Ibid.

11. Julius Barnes, DBC memorandum, J. D. Mahoney Scrapbook, Duluth Boat Club records, NEMHC S3009.

12. Gil Fawcett (television script), KDAL-TV, August 24, 1955.

13. Interview with Henning E. Peterson.

14. DBC memorandum, May 31, 1909, J. D. Mahoney Scrapbook, Duluth Boat Club records, NEMHC S3009.

15. DBC memorandum, undated, J. D. Mahoney Scrapbook, Duluth Boat Club records, NEMHC S3009.

16. Gil Fawcett (television script), KDAL-TV, August 24, 1955.

17. *Duluth News Tribune*, July 21, 1911, pp. 1–3.

18. DBC memorandum, circa 1911, J. D. Mahoney Scrapbook, Duluth Boat Club records, NEMHC S3009.

19. *Duluth News Tribune*, July 21, 1911, p. 1.

20. DBC Pamphlet, 1911, from the J. D. Mahoney Scrapbook, Duluth Boat Club records, NEMHC S3009.

21. *Duluth News Tribune*, July 22, 1911, pp. 1–2.

22. *Duluth News Tribune*, July 23, 1911, editorial page.

23. DBC memorandum, August 30 (no year given), circa 1911, from the J. D. Mahoney Scrapbook, Duluth Boat Club records, NEMHC S3009.

24. DBC memorandum, June 11, 1908, J. D. Mahoney Scrapbook, Duluth Boat Club records, NEMHC S3009.

25. DBC memorandum, undated, J. D. Mahoney Scrapbook, Duluth Boat Club records, NEMHC S3009.

26. DBC memorandum, undated, J. D. Mahoney Scrapbook, Duluth Boat Club records, NEMHC S3009.

27. DBC memorandum, circa 1912, J. D. Mahoney Scrapbook, Duluth Boat Club records, NEMHC S3009.

28. *Duluth Herald*, July 12, 1925, p. 10.

29. Sailing Regulations, DBC Pamphlet, 1912, from the J. D. Mahoney Scrapbook, Duluth Boat Club records, NEMHC S3009.

30. Duluth Boat Club Yearbook 1913, Duluth Boat Club records, NEMHC S3009.

31. DBC Log 1917, vol. 3, no. 3, May and June, 1917, DBC Files, NEMHC.

32. Duluth Boat Club Yearbook 1913, op. cit.

33. Ibid.

34. Riverside Review, August 1919, Julius H. Barnes Papers, NEMHC S3025.

35. DBC memorandum, June 25, 1908, J. D. Mahoney Scrapbook, Duluth Boat Club records, NEMHC S3009.

36. DBC memorandum, undated, J. D. Mahoney Scrapbook, Duluth Boat Club records, NEMHC S3009.

37. DBC memorandum, circa 1911, J. D. Mahoney Scrapbook, Duluth Boat Club records, NEMHC S3009.

38. DBC memorandum, circa 1916, J. D. Mahoney Scrapbook, Duluth Boat Club records, NEMHC S3009.

39. Letter to members of the Duluth Boat Club, April 25, 1916, J. D. Mahoney Scrapbook, Duluth Boat Club records, NEMHC S3009.

40. Interview with Henning E. Peterson, September 6, 1971.

41. *DBC Log 1917*, vol. 3, no. 3, May and June, 1917, DBC Files, NEMHC.

42. *Duluth News Tribune*, August 10, 1916, pp. 1–2.

43. Ibid.

44. *Duluth News Tribune*, August 14, 1916, editorial, p. 4.

45. *DBC Log 1917*, vol. 3, no. 3, May and June, 1917, DBC Files, NEMHC.

46. Letter from the Duluth Water Sports Center, May 23, 1931, Duluth Boat Club records, NEMHC S3009.

47. International Swimming Hall of Fame Biography, http://www.ishof.org/honorees/65/65mmann.html.

48. Alison McBean Buckingham interview, n.d., NEMHC S2250 tape 28.

49. *Duluth News Tribune*, July 21, 1925, p. 16.

50. Unidentified newspaper clipping from the DBC Files, Duluth Boat Club records, NEMHC S3009.

51. *New York Times*, September 7, 1920.

52. *DBC Log 1917*, vol. 6, August 1920, Duluth Boat Club records, NEMHC S3009.

53. Buckingham recording, op. cit.

*NEMHC refers to the Northeast Minnesota Historical Center, archives of the St. Louis County Historical Society.

CHAPTER 3

the invincible era

During the latter part of the nineteenth century, the Minnesota-Winnipeg Rowing Association had its regattas curtailed by the Spanish-American War and the Boer War, which together drained oarsmen from both the American and Canadian clubs. However, it was squabbling between clubs that ended the association altogether. The Minnesota Boat Club complained that Rat Portage was competing with professional oarsmen. They insisted that Rat Portage be thrown out of the association, or they, the Minnesota Boat Club, would withdraw. Winnipeg sided with Rat Portage, denying the claims of professionalism and threatened to withdraw if Rat Portage was ousted.[1] This dispute was never settled, and the annual regattas, which were suspended because of the war anyway, were not held again.

However, area rowing did not cease altogether with the last Minnesota-Winnipeg Association Regatta on Lake Minnetonka in 1897. The Minnesota and Rat Portage clubs each won a race in the U.S. National Regatta, while Winnipeg won seven Canadian and six U.S. national championship races, and their four-oared crew won the Stewards Challenge Cup at the British Henley Regatta in England, which symbolized world supremacy in that event.[2] In Duluth, there was no competitive rowing at this time.

In 1905, the Winnipeg, Minnesota, and Duluth clubs decided to form another rowing association, to be called the Minnesota and West Canada Rowing Association. Its first regatta was held in 1906, with the Fort William Rowing Club from Ontario also represented.[3]

This regatta represented the first real competition for Duluth oarsmen in nine years. In the interlude, some club members continued to row and scull for exercise, but there was no competitive racing with other clubs. Despite this long layoff, the regatta of 1906 was a successful one for the Duluth Boat Club. Duluth won both the junior four and eight events, but came in behind the powerful Saint Paul and Winnipeg crews in the senior eight race.[4]

This promising start in the new association, which changed its name to the North-Western International Rowing Association in 1909,[5] was to be followed by disappointment for the next four years. During the period 1907–1910, the Duluth Boat Club was

Amateur rowing became even more popular during the early part of the twentieth century. Rowing was frequently seen on the covers of a variety of magazines, as shown here.

52

CHAPTER 3: THE INVINCIBLE ERA

unable to win a single victory, despite the fact that the club switched from amateur to professional coaching when Julius Barnes hired Wisconsin crew coach Andy O'Dea to coach the Duluth crews in the summer.

Barnes paid the coach's salary out of his own pocket. He very much wanted to see the Duluth Boat Club become a top rowing power. Barnes's sentiments toward rowing were expressed in the Duluth Boat Club yearbook of 1908:

The club believes in rowing and rowing races. It is the cleanest sport in the world; the one most free from professionalism; the one that most surely teaches youth the value of continued hard exertion, the persistent determination that finally wins success from apparent defeat, and the value of discipline and self-control.[6]

During this winless period, the Duluth Boat Club had the best equipment in the association, they had hired a professional coach, and the oarsmen were among the better athletes in town, yet they lost. The Duluth oarsmen had a difficult challenge because the North-Western Rowing Association was one of the most formidable rowing associations in North America.

Barnes used a tactic popular among the owners of professional athletic teams when they are struggling; he decided that what the club needed was a new coach. Choosing not to rehire O'Dea, Barnes brought James A. (Jimmie) Ten Eyck to coach at Duluth. Ten Eyck was one of the most prestigious names in rowing history. J. A. Ten Eyck was the son of James E. Ten Eyck, a famous professional sculler, who attained even greater renown as a very successful crew coach at the University of Syracuse. J. A. Ten Eyck was also the brother of Edward Hanlon (Ned) Ten Eyck, who achieved fame by being the first American to win the coveted Diamond Sculls, symbolic of world amateur championship in the single sculls, at the Royal British Henley Regatta at the young age of seventeen. Ned Ten Eyck later became a professional oarsman like his father. J. A. Ten Eyck made his name in rowing by stroking championship crews

James E. Ten Eyck (young Jim) and Edward Hanlon (Ned) Ten Eyck were the primary coaches for the Duluth Boat Club during the glory years and were ably assisted by their famous father. Ned Ten Eyck had the distinction of being the first American and youngest sculler (at age seventeen) to win the Diamond Sculls at the British Royal Henley Regatta in England. Winning this race was emblematic of the world rowing championship in the single sculls.

NEMHC 52422 b5f1

James A. Ten Eyck, former professional sculler and head coach at the University of Syracuse, would coach the Duluth Boat Club with his sons during the summer. He was one of the most successful and famous college rowing coaches. Recruiting experienced Duluth Boat Club oarsmen to row at Syracuse helped his success.

NEMHC 52422 b5f3

INVINCIBLE: HISTORY OF THE DULUTH BOAT CLUB

at the University of Syracuse under his father's tutelage, but his real distinction would come from the records established by the Duluth Boat Club under his coaching.

In his first year of coaching, Ten Eyck trained his crews intensively, producing improvement that was noticeable to an observer, and brought results that were slightly better than before. In the North-Western Regatta held in Duluth in 1911, the only race won by the Duluth Boat Club was the bantam-four event, a race for lightweight oarsmen weighing 142 pounds or less. This was a pleasant surprise for knowledgeable followers of Duluth rowing, who expected that the bantams would not be quite as likely to win as the junior eight, which lost. The eights made a respectable showing in spite of their defeat,

Duluth Boat Club Junior Four 1912 (in boat). NWIRA Junior Four winners.

taking second places behind the great crews of Winnipeg, giving them a close race all the way.[7] The results were encouraging enough that upon hearing that, for various reasons, Winnipeg would not be entering competition in the U.S. National Regatta, the officers of the boat club decided to send an eight out east to find out how their oarsmen would compare with the competition in the Nationals. Duluth took a second at this regatta, and it was consequently discovered that they were developing a caliber of rowing that compared favorably with the best.[8]

In 1912, the ability of Duluth's rowers was demonstrated more concretely. Besides winning the bantam-four at the North-Western Regatta again, the Duluth Boat Club also won the junior and senior eight races. At the National Regatta in Peoria, Illinois, the Duluth Boat Club won the intermediate eight race (intermediate being a category for crews that have only won junior races, a status higher than junior and less than senior) in record time. In the senior eight race, Duluth lost to their old nemesis, Winnipeg, by only one-fourth of a boat length. Since Duluth crossed the finish line well ahead of the senior eight from the Detroit Boat Club, which had defeated the best eastern competition, Duluthians felt justified in saying that their city

Duluth Boat Club Bantam Four 1912. NWIRA winners. Three of these rowers would form the Invincible Four and never lose a race.

NEMHC big photos

54

CHAPTER 3: THE INVINCIBLE ERA

possessed the eight best oarsmen in the United States. For their efforts, the Duluth Boat Club oarsmen were greeted upon their return by a large crowd and a band, which led them on a parade through a cheering city.[9]

By 1913, Duluth rowing fans could claim that their oarsmen were the best without any caveats. The Duluth Boat Club dominated the North-Western Regatta and went on to be the most impressive club at the National Regatta in Boston, winning four races: the intermediate fours and eights and the senior fours and eights.[10] Special significance was given to this feat by the fact that there were four men that rowed in all four races. Usually, an oarsman trains for just one or two events for a championship regatta. A single hard-contested rowing contest is normally enough to completely exhaust even a well-conditioned individual. An individual winning four sweep medals in one National Regatta is a very rare occurrence. This feat was rather amazing since all four oarsmen were small and lightweight. They averaged 148 pounds, and their average age was only twenty years. Since size and experience are thought to be as important in rowing as in many other sports (all things being equal, the bigger men should win), these victories demonstrated exceptional effort and ability. These four men were Dave Horak (stroke), Doug Moore, Max Rheinberger, and Phil Moore (bow), brother of Doug. These four became referred to in the newspapers as the Invincible Four.

1913 Champions of America. This team became known as the Invincible Four, eventually winning twenty-two races in national and international regattas and retiring undefeated after four years of competition.

NEMHC S2386 "O" box 56

55

INVINCIBLE: HISTORY OF THE DULUTH BOAT CLUB

1913 Champion Eight. This crew won the Junior Eight at the NWIRA and both the Intermediate and Senior Eight Races at the National Championships in Boston. NEMHC S2386 "O" box 56

In 1914, the Duluth Boat Club won even more races than they did the year before. At the National Regatta in Philadelphia, Duluth oarsmen won the intermediate double, four and eight. The Invincible Four won the senior four race again and rowed in the victorious senior eight. The rowing enthusiasts in the East were very much impressed, as the following excerpt from a story in the *Philadelphia Ledger* shows:

> *James A. Ten Eyck, a worthy son of a worthy father, coaches the oarsmen of the Duluth Boat Club, the largest organization of its kind in the world. Ten Eyck brought a navy of oars to this city for the 42nd annual national championship, which was held on the Schuylkill Friday and Saturday last, and returned to Duluth with five distinct victories. The nation can be proud of such a body of men. They are a credit to the rowing world. Very few rowing clubs in America can show such a record for any one championship regatta.*[11]

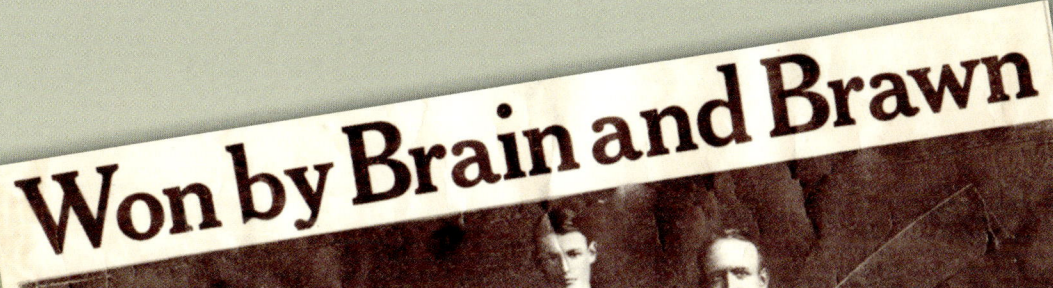

This advertisement for Shredded Wheat says it all.

NEMHC S2386 "O" box 56

If people thought that the accomplishments of Duluth's 1914 crews would stand long unsurpassed, they were wrong. In 1915, the Duluth Boat Club had the greatest success that a club would ever have at a national championship regatta. The *New York Times* carried an article that gave a good condensation of the whole story.[12]

The Duluth Boat Club demonstrated its remarkable rowing supremacy in this country in a surprising manner at the annual regatta of the National Association of Amateur Oarsmen, which ended on the Connecticut River today. The blue-jerseyed pupils of young Jim Ten Eyck went home with ten firsts and one second to their credit, the spoils of the eleven events in which they were entered.

This performance is something unheard of in the history of amateur rowing. The feat was accomplished with a squad of 34 oarsmen, after a long trip from Minnesota.

The Invincible Four in 1914 poses on the water. From left, Dave Horak, Doug Moore, Max Rheinberger, Phil Moore. These men started rowing as 142-pound bantamweight rowers and during their entire rowing career never had a problem defeating much bigger, stronger men.
NEMHC S2386 "O" box 56

Four of the Duluth crews established new association records during the afternoon. The senior fours rowed in 6:14 3/5, compared with 6:27 4/5 made by the New York Athletic Club at Detroit in 1909. In the quadruple race, the Duluth crew covered the course in 5:45 4/5 as against 7:07 4/5, made by the Riversides in Boston in 1913. The Duluth intermediate eight swept down the river in 5:35 4/5, the old time being 6:03, made by the Argos at Detroit in 1900. The senior Duluth eight closed the record-breaking day by rowing the course in 5:30 3/5. The former time was 6:05 made by the NYAC at Detroit in 1900.

This same *Times* article also mentioned that Duluth oarsmen had broken records during the first day of the regatta also. The junior eight posted a record time of 5:55, and Duluth's single sculler, Walter Hoover, lowered the record in the single quarter-mile dash from 1:16 to 1:08. At the conclusion of the National Regatta of 1915, the Duluth Boat Club

CHAPTER 3: THE INVINCIBLE ERA

The national championship senior eight from 1914. From left, coxswain Lincoln Brown, Dave Horak, Doug Moore, Roy Kent, Wallace Quimby, Walter Hoover, Walter Beschenbossel, Max Rheinberger, and Phil Moore. Photo from the Duluth Public Library Slide Collection. "Persons seeing the Duluth crews for the first time often remarked how unlike athletes some of the men appeared until they stepped into a scull. A few were tall and skinny, while others were short and stocky. But they fit into a boat like cogs in a wheel and operated as smoothly."—*Springfield Daily Republic*, August 14, 1915.

had broken or held the record time for nearly every event in rowing. The one-and-one-quarter-mile single race was an exception. The records were made on the Connecticut River, which had an estimated current of one mile per hour.[13]

These times can only be speculatively compared with times from other regattas because wind and current can have a considerable impact on race time and vary so greatly from different venues or even races on different dates on the same venue. However, some of the races were raced around stakes or buoys. In the 1915 National Championships, the single and the senior four races were rowed with a turn (although the senior international four was rowed straight away).

In 1914 at the U.S. National Championship Regatta in Philadelphia, Duluth oarsmen won the Intermediate Double, Intermediate Four, Intermediate Eight, the International Senior Four Race, and the Senior Eight. The Duluth oarsmen won the following accolade from the Public Ledger-Philadelphia, August 10, 1914: "The nation can be proud of such a body of men. They are a credit to the rowing world. Very few rowing clubs in America can show such a record for any one championship regatta."

NEMHC S2386 "O" box 56

" Training was both Spartan and puritanical. As soon as the ice went out in the spring we moved down to the Point and into the living quarters provided by the club for its galley slaves. The trainers looked on women as a menace and took every precaution to protect us from their depredations. We were released during school and working hours. Otherwise we lived a life of poverty, chastity, and obedience, with special emphasis on the mortification of the flesh. " —John L. Peyton in a somewhat sardonic reminiscence about his experience as a rower in the Duluth Boat Club from his book *Bright Beat the Water – Memories of a Wilderness Artist*, 1993, by the McDonald & Woodward Publishing Company.

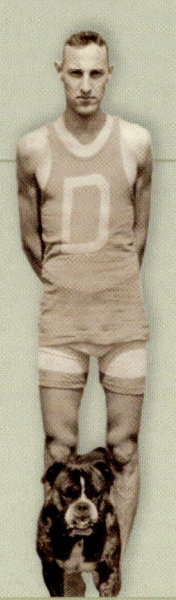

At the 1916 Nationals, the senior four race was also rowed with a turn. In a turning race, the oarsmen row half of the entire distance (one and one-quarter miles, in this case), then they make a 180-degree turn around a stake or buoy and return back the way they came, finishing where they started. Racing with a turn has long since fallen from practice and the oar-handling skill required to turn a stake has become a lost art. Observers remarked that Duluth's Invincible Four were so adept with their blade work that they could turn a stake and be heading for the finish line at full speed in a matter of seconds.[14]

The easterners had greeted the Duluth Boat Club's first success with surprise and respect, but they eventually found Duluth's superiority to be somewhat aggravating. Suspicions and grumblings started, concerning "an endowed club" and "hired oarsmen."[15] It seemed to them that such mastery showed an obvious difference between the crews of the Duluth Boat Club and those of other clubs, and some thought that such a difference represented that which exists between amateurs and professionals. Those who were gracious enough not to accuse the Duluth Boat Club of professionalism still found the redundancy of their victories rather tiring. The latter attitude seemed to have been conveyed in the following excerpt from an article from the *Springfield Daily Republic*.

> *It was the same old thing over and over again. Duluth oarsmen started the afternoon of the first day's program of the 43rd annual regatta of the National Association of Amateur Oarsmen yesterday at Riverside Parkway winning, and they kept everlastingly at it, right through to the finish of the card.*
>
> *They won everything in sight, won every event in which they started and there were six of them. Crack crews from Boston, Philadelphia, Detroit and New York all tried to break up the winning streak of the Lake Superior water wonders, and they all failed. It didn't make any difference what kind of race Duluth entered; the result was always the same. The Duluth blue waved everywhere.*[16]

The accusation of professionalism was inaccurate. The Duluth oarsmen were not professionals since they all had jobs and none of them received any money for their rowing. They were native Duluthians and not talented athletes imported from somewhere else. But, the Duluth Boat Club rowing program was endowed. Although initiation fees and membership dues financed the general activities of the boat club, the rowing expenses were completely paid for by Julius H. Barnes. He paid the coaches, bought the shells, and paid all the expenses of the costly trips east to the national regattas. An article in the *Duluth Herald* noted that Barnes was perhaps the greatest single factor in the rowing success of the Duluth Boat Club.

> *Mr. Barnes has made possible these great victories of the past through his perseverance and faith in local rowing.*
>
> *It has been through Mr. Barnes' financial help that Duluth was able to receive the senior services of Ten Eyck, as well as the splendid rowing equipment of which the club is now possessed.*
>
> *In thirty years of rowing previous to 1911 and the engaging of Jimmie Ten Eyck as rowing coach, we had won but four victories—three junior fours and a junior eight in the North-Western Association. We were practically unheard of as far as rowing was concerned, outside of our own state.*[17]

The Duluth Boat Club owned the most and best rowing equipment of any rowing organization in the United States.[18] Not only did Barnes buy the best shells available, he also replaced the racing equipment every year. Barnes would have the racing shells transported to the National Regatta in a railroad baggage car. When the regatta was over, all the shells would be sold at half-price to interested clubs, and the Duluth Boat Club would begin the next year with a complete set of new boats.[19]

In an interview, Henning E. Peterson described the trips to the 1919 and 1920 regattas. This is probably representative of what the other trips were like. For the trip east, Barnes rented a private sleeper coach for the oarsmen, coaches, and boatman; a baggage car for the shells; and a motor launch for the coach. Several barrels of pure Lake Superior drinking water were brought along to ensure that the oarsmen were not contaminated by foreign drinking water that their bodies would not have time to adjust to. The oarsmen all stayed in a single large hotel during the regatta and the preceding week, and they were not allowed to leave their room, except for either daily rowing practice or the races. Barnes paid for all lodging and meals, up till the last day of the regatta. He even rented a bus to drive the oarsmen from the hotel to the boathouse and back every day. Since the oarsmen needed a week to become used to the body of water that the regatta was to be held on, they would be gone a total of two weeks for a two-day regatta. Barnes paid for every expense for the entire duration.[20]

RACING SHELLS FOR SALE

The Duluth Boat Club offer for sale their complete equipment of new sectional racing shells. Because of the expense of transporting these shells back to Duluth it will be more reasonable to dispose of them at low prices during the National Regatta at Philadelphia. Every boat is in perfect condition, being used only three months.

Two Sectional Eights at $400.00 each.
Two Sectional Fours at $200.00 each.
One Solid Four, three seasons old at $150.00.
One new Single Shell at $80.00.

Full information may be had from
J. E. TEN EYCK,
Duluth Boat Club Rowing Coach.

Barnes paying for equipment and traveling expenses helped the rowing success of the Duluth Boat Club considerably, but the real key to their accomplishments was the way that they trained, a result of Ten Eyck's coaching. Every year, Ten Eyck began training his men indoors on rowing machines on March 1. Indoor training was essential because the ice in the Duluth-Superior harbor was still several feet thick in March, while crews in the east had open water most of the year and were usually out rowing by March. In addition to working out on the rowing machines, the oarsmen would do setting up exercises and run three miles every day to build up their wind and legs. The indoor workouts would continue until the ice in the harbor broke up, upon when they started rowing on the water. They would be rowing while ice hunks were floating about them, and because the temperature was sometimes below freezing, the riggers and oars were often encrusted with a coat of ice.[21] Because the Duluth Boat Club knew that other clubs had a head start on them, they could not wait for warmer weather to begin rowing.

Sometime around the first week in May, training would begin in earnest. The oarsmen would eat and sleep at the boat club from that date until the end of the season. This was to ensure that a demanding regimen would be strictly followed. The coach could keep a watchful eye on them and make sure that they were in bed by 10:00 p.m. every night. They needed to be well rested because they were awakened at 6:00 a.m. and out on the water rowing by 6:15. No alarm clocks were necessary. The coach rousted the crew by pounding on the side of the bunkhouse with a baseball bat. After a relatively short morning row, the oarsmen would eat breakfast at the club and then go to work. The hard workout

Duluth rowers get in an early spring practice. In the background is a sheet of ice with an iceboat gliding over it.

From The Zenith, *July 1916, from the personal collection of David Bjorkman*

INVINCIBLE: HISTORY OF THE DULUTH BOAT CLUB

The weather in Duluth could be brutal in the spring (and still can be), as shown in this photo of a coach in full rain gear.

NEMHC 52422 b5f3

would begin at 5:00 p.m. after the rowers had returned from their jobs. For the first two months on the water, the oarsmen rowed ten to twenty hard, steady miles per day over the two workouts. During the last six weeks, the workouts were focused on the mile and a quarter racing distance, practicing long sprints and starts.

Several eights, fours, and doubles would go out together with Ten Eyck alongside in a motor launch pointing out any mistakes and noticing who worked the hardest. Every evening practice ended with a race among all the boats. They were given handicaps according to speed, with the slower boats receiving a head start. Every boat had a chance of finishing first if its crewmembers gave it all they had.[22]

After their workout, the oarsmen would eat supper at the boat club. Eating meals at the club gave the men little opportunity to stray from the strict diet, which was an integral part of their conditioning. All fried foods were prohibited, except steaks fried in butter for some unexplained reason. Pork, veal, ham, liver, corned beef, and fish were forbidden, along with hash, boiled and pressed meats, stews, and soup. Most vegetables were acceptable, except onions, beets, rhubarb, beans in any form, lettuce, radishes, cabbage, and boiled or fried potatoes. Poached and medium-boiled eggs were recommended, while fried or hard-boiled eggs were not allowed. Fresh bread and pastry was taboo, but stale bread or toast was acceptable. Milk, coffee, tea, all soft drinks, and any drink with ice in it, including ice water, were excluded from the diet. The only permissible drinks were plain water and cocoa. Bananas and over-ripe fruit of any kind were forbidden, as were colored ice cream and candy. Proper food for oarsmen, according to the Duluth Boat Club diet, consisted of steaks, roast beef, lamb and chicken, all vegetables except those mentioned as not being beneficial, poached or medium-boiled eggs, stale bread or toast, cocoa, shredded wheat and cereals, custard, rice pudding, prunes, apricots, tapioca, and vanilla ice cream with meals or at night in moderation.[23]

The diet was a vital part of the entire training regimen. The oarsmen had faith in their coach and followed the diet just as they followed the demanding workouts.[24] The result was not only a tough physical constitution, but also a tough mental attitude. They were supremely confident that their bodies were in perfect tune for a rowing contest. When the Duluth men were at the starting line waiting for the beginning of a race, they had no uncertainties about their preparation for the race. They believed they had followed the best of all possible training programs.

The accomplishments of the training regimen are evident in photographs of the Duluth Boat Club oarsmen. The oarsmen show a high degree of muscle tone and definition. There is no visible fat. They are well muscled but not bulky. Muscular strength was not increased beyond its rowing function.

The diet was just part of the entire regimen, which encompassed nearly every aspect of the oarsmen's lives. The lives of these men were regulated by a never-changing schedule. They woke, ate, worked, rowed, and slept at exactly the same time every day. Ten Eyck also told his trainees that they would have to "stay away from the girls during the rowing season."[25]

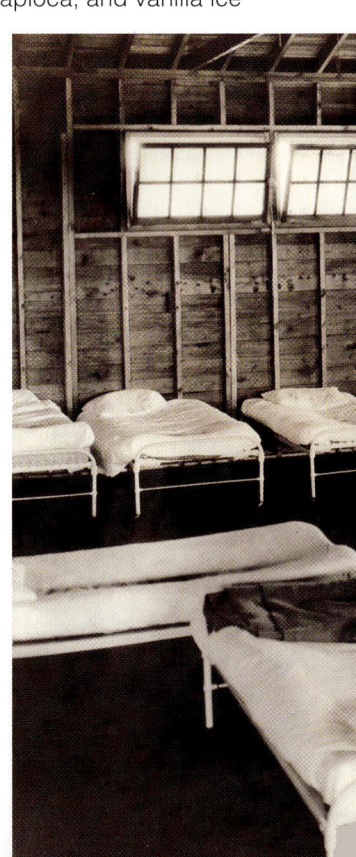

CHAPTER 3: THE INVINCIBLE ERA

This last regulation was not as difficult to enforce since the oarsmen all slept together in a dormitory that the Duluth Boat Club built specifically for this purpose. The bunkhouse was one large open room, so it would be hard for a rower to break training by staying out late and partying without others knowing about it. Those who broke these training rules were out of the crew no matter how good they were. Even missing practice because of illness was not an excuse.

Complete commitment is one answer to the question of why the Duluth Boat Club crews were so successful, but it is no coincidence that the total dedication and the success did not commence until large sums of money were spent on the club's rowing program. First of all, the entire training program was designed by the Ten Eycks, who were paid to coach at the Duluth Boat Club by Julius Barnes. Once the training program was designed, it took a substantial amount of money to carry it out. The only way to ensure that the oarsmen followed their diet was to cook and serve their meals for them right at the boat club. The way to make sure that the oarsmen received proper rest was to have them all sleep right at the boat club, which also kept them from other temptations that weren't part of the training program. These measures also made more rowing time possible, since the oarsmen did not need to spend time cooking, washing dishes, or traveling between home and the boat club. The club built a dormitory, kitchen, and dining room for the oarsmen and hired a cook and a housekeeper.

The oarsmen's dining hall at the Duluth Boat Club. The meals served here followed the strict training diet for the oarsmen.
NEMHC 52422 b5f2

The oarsmen at the Duluth Boat Club slept in this bunkhouse. All lights were out at 10:00 p.m. Rise and shine at 6:00 a.m. NEMHC 52422 b5f2

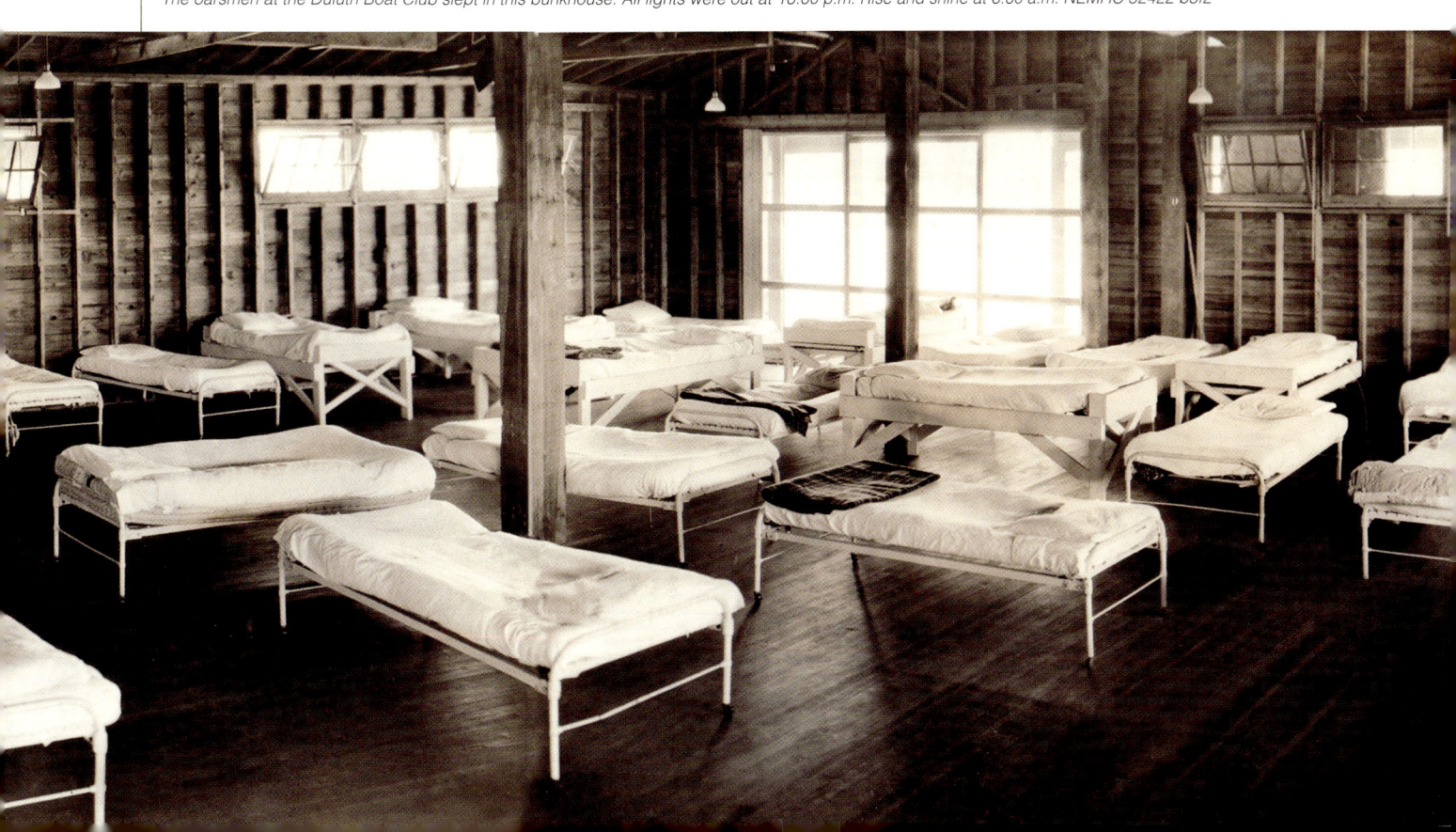

The oarsmen paid the cost of their board themselves—$4.00 per week before World War I, $4.50 in 1917 and 1918,[26] and $7.00 per week thereafter.[27] This seemingly small amount probably did cover all room and board costs. The oarsmen were always able to eat as much as they wished, and they frequently feasted on beefsteak, but the cost of food and services was low during this period. For example, the payroll of the Duluth Boat Club's Main Café for August 1916 shows that wages ranged from $3.33 per day for the head chef to $1.00 per day for waiters and dishwashers.[28] Because the cost of food was also low, the Main Café could sell a rather elaborate supper for fifty cents.[29]

The candidates for Duluth Crew were usually high school boys, boys learning a trade, office men, and clerks. They all had to be amateurs, which meant that they could not receive money for playing or teaching any kind of sport and they could not be engaged in commercial rowing such as ferrying. Oarsmen seldom had problems finding jobs that had a work schedule compatible with rowing since there were club members willing to help them obtain such jobs. In 1914, a majority of the oarsmen were employed as clerks, mostly in municipal offices.[30] Since many of Duluth's civic and business leaders belonged to the boat club, it was a very simple matter to provide jobs for those who rowed.

Another factor that led to bitterness and accusations of professionalism against the Duluth Boat Club was the fact that many of the oarsmen trained by J. A. Ten Eyck at Duluth would later attend the University of Syracuse and row there under the coaching of his father, J. E. Ten Eyck. Syracuse, at this time, was annually a top collegiate rowing power in

A photograph of the 1916 collegiate varsity champions from Syracuse University. Half of the crew was from Duluth. Whiteside (second from left), Williams (third from left), Osman (sixth from left), and Glass (eighth from left) rowed for the Duluth Boat Club before entering college.

Collection of Brian Stoll (grandson of Art Osman)

the nation. In 1916, the Syracuse varsity eight went undefeated and won the intercollegiate rowing championship in a four-mile race at Poughkeepsie with four Duluth oarsmen in the crew.

Other colleges displayed a degree of acrimony toward Syracuse because the latter had the advantage of having some of their oarsmen trained even before their freshmen year. The following article from the *Duluth News Tribune* gives a good picture of what was happening:[31]

> *The boys who have passed from the tutelage of "Young Jim" Ten Eyck at Duluth to that of "Old Jim" Ten Eyck have won a lot of glory for Syracuse University, but have made considerable trouble also. The Duluth boys have proved so good that other universities have tried to handicap Syracuse on account of their presence—and with some success.*
>
> *This year, the rule of the intercollegiate regatta stewards that no former club oarsmen may row in the freshman crews at all, or in the varsity crews unless they can show one-year residence at their college will be strictly*

CHAPTER 3: THE INVINCIBLE ERA

enforced. The rule is aimed at Syracuse because of the Duluth boys and is framed by Penn, Cornell and Columbia, who control the regatta.

After the rowing success of 1913, 1914, and 1915, the Duluth Boat Club felt that it was entitled to host the next regatta of the National Association of Amateur Oarsmen. To convince the officers of the NAAO that Duluth could and would support such a regatta, Julius Barnes presented them with a petition bearing the signatures of ten thousand Duluthians asking that the National Regatta be held in Duluth.[32] Since Duluth is a long distance away from the rowing centers in Philadelphia, Boston, and New York, Julius Barnes agreed to pay for the transportation of all eastern oarsmen as far as Chicago.[33] Trophies and medals were promised to winning oarsmen, and Barnes added that he would present the National Association with an expensive traveling trophy, to be awarded annually to the rowing club that made the strongest overall showing in the National Regatta. In view of the unusual efforts made by Barnes and the rest of the Duluth contingent to secure the National Regatta for their city, the officers of the NAAO could hardly refuse, and they didn't.

The Barnes Trophy presented by Julius Barnes to the National Association of Amateur Oarsmen in 1916 to be awarded annually to the grand aggregate point total winner for overall best performance in the annual U.S. National Championship Regatta. The winner of the Barnes Trophy was determined on the basis of a point system that Barnes devised. The Barnes trophy is still contended for at the annual American Rowing Championships. Photograph courtesy of the U.S. Rowing Association.

Detail from the same photograph of the Barnes trophy.

67

A poster stamp used to advertise the 1916 National Rowing Championships and Water Carnival held in Duluth. The event put on by the Duluth Boat Club was highly praised by the National Association of Amateur Oarsmen as being the finest ever held in the history of the NAAO.

Image from the collection of Kerry Ahearn

These gentlemen from the Duluth Boat Club formed the National Regatta Committee responsible for hosting the National Championship Rowing Regatta held in Duluth in 1916.

NEMHC 52422 b5f1

Right: The banner for the National Association of Amateur Oarsmen (NAAO) Senior Eight Championship in 1916.

Photo by Bruce Ojard Photographics

Left: The trophy presented to the winning senior eight at the 1916 National Championships is now part of the collection of the Saint Louis County Historical Society.

Photograph by Bruce Ojard

The crew that won the senior quad event at the 1916 National Championships in Duluth.

Image obtained from KJS Consulting

A photograph of the national championship senior eight race at Duluth in 1916. Duluth is in the lead and would increase the lead shown here by two lengths at the finish. The Undine Barge Club of Philadelphia would take second, followed by the Detroit Boat Club. The New York Athletic Club led the second group of boats to take fourth place ahead of the Farragut Boat Club of Lynn, Massachusetts, and the Minnesota Boat Club of St. Paul.

Duluth Public Library slides

The news that the National Regatta would be held in Duluth in 1916 was met with tremendous excitement by the people of the city. The enthusiasm of the citizens of Duluth was paralleled by the preparations that Julius Barnes and the boat club made for the regatta. The officers of the National Association of Amateur Oarsmen were very impressed. Robert H. L. Peton, secretary of that organization, stated, "The 1916 National Regatta surpasses all previous ones, both in the numbers of entries and in the arrangements which have been made for the comfort and accommodation of both oarsmen and spectators." James Pilkington, president of the NAAC, said nearly the same thing, "Of all the regattas I have attended, I have never seen the equal of the accommodations provided by the Duluth Boat Club for both oarsmen and visitors."[34]

The hospitality of the Duluth Boat Club did not extend so far as to include the rowing itself. The home club won nine out of twelve events entered; the junior eight, intermediate double, intermediate four, intermediate eight, senior double, senior four, senior international four, senior quad, and senior eight. Duluth won the Barnes Trophy for overall showing with four times as many points as their closest competitor, the Undine Barge Club of Philadelphia. The role of training in these victories was evident since not a single Duluth man collapsed from exhaustion after the races, as many oarsmen from other clubs did.[35]

One of the highlights of the regatta was the senior doubles race featuring the famous scullers from the Vesper Boat Club of Philadelphia, John B. Kelly and his cousin Paul Costello. Racing against the formidable Vespers were the

"Duluth giants," Roy Kent and A. E. Osman, so named because they were two of the biggest and strongest oarsmen ever to row for Duluth. The race was not close. The big Duluth scullers took the lead at the start of the race and increased it enough through the body of the race so that the tremendous finishing sprint of the Vespers still left them a length behind the Duluthians at the end.[36] That is the newspaper version of the race, but legend has it that during the race Kent taunted the Vesper team by coaching them down the course, until they got near the end and said, "See you Kelly," and left them behind. This was the second time that Jack Kelly lost to Kent and Osman in a championship double race. In the 1915 national championship regatta in Springfield, Kelly and Waldo Smith (another national single sculling champion) lost to the "Duluth giants." Kelly and Costello fared much better after Kent and Osman retired from rowing.

The water carnival of 1916 was such a success that many people advocated making it an annual municipal celebration, financed by contributions to a carnival fund. Such plans were thwarted by America's entry into World War I. The National Regatta was cancelled during 1917 and 1918. Most of Duluth's champion oarsmen entered the armed forces, permanently terminating their competitive rowing.

The war did not stop rowing at the Duluth Boat Club altogether, as high school students and even younger boys filled the places of those who were in the service. Training continued in full force, with young oarsmen living and practicing daily at the club. During 1917 and 1918, there was not just one, but three Ten Eycks coaching at the Duluth Boat Club. Young Jimmie Ten Eyck was joined by his brother Ned and his father, "Old Jim," who started to spend his summers in Duluth while still coaching the University of Syracuse crews during the school year. Since there were no regattas being held, all of the oarsmen were divided into three distinct units, each of which coached by a different Ten Eyck. These units, which were designed to be of equal ability, behaved like individual clubs. The training was done separately, with

JACK KELLY

DEFEATED BY ART OSMAN AND ROY KENT FROM THE DULUTH BOAT CLUB IN THE DOUBLE SCULLS AT THE U.S. NATIONALS IN 1915 AND 1916

John B. Kelly Sr., also known as Jack Kelly, was one of the most accomplished oarsman in the history of rowing. He was a triple Olympic gold medal winner and won 126 straight races in the single scull.

At the time he won his races, rowing was at the height of its popularity. Kelly's exploits were well covered in newsprint. In many ways, he was a figure comparable to Babe Ruth or Jack Dempsey.

Kelly began his business career as a bricklayer in Philadelphia, and he learned to row on the Schuylkill River in 1908.

Kelly represented the United States at the 1920 Summer Olympics in Antwerp, Belgium. In a hard-fought race, he won the single scull event by defeating the winner of the Diamond Sculls, British sculler Jack Beresford. Half an hour after the singles final, Kelly teamed with his cousin Paul Costello to win the double scull (2x) race, a feat that has never been repeated at the Olympic games.

In 1924, Kelly and Costello repeated their success, winning the double scull event at the Summer Olympics in Paris.

Philadelphia erected a prominent statue of Kelly near the finish line of the Schuylkill River course that Kelly rowed. It is located just off scenic "Kelly Drive," which is named for Kelly's son, Jack Jr. Every year, USRowing bestows the Jack Kelly Award on an individual who represents the ideals that Jack Kelly exemplified, including superior achievement in rowing, service to amateur athletics, and success in his or her chosen profession.

Source: http://en.wikipedia.org/wiki/John_B._Kelly,_Sr.

Jack Kelly in his single on the Schuylkill River in Philadelphia.
Image from http://en.wikipedia.org/wiki/John_B._Kelly,_Sr

Statue of John B. Kelly Sr., which is located on "Kelly Drive" along the Schuykill River in Philadelphia.
Image from http://en.wikipedia.org/wiki/John_B._Kelly,_Sr.

PAUL COSTELLO
DEFEATED BY WALTER HOOVER FOR THE PHILADELPHIA GOLD CHALLENGE CUP IN 1922

Drawing of the triple Olympic gold medal winner Paul Costello.
Image taken from the North American, *Philadelphia, Sunday, August 6, 1922*

Paul Costello was an American triple Olympic gold medal winner in rowing, and he was the first person to win a gold medal in the same event, the double scull (2x), at three consecutive Olympics. He also won numerous national titles in both the single and double scull in the 1920s.

Costello won the double scull race with his cousin Jack Kelly at the 1920 Olympics in Antwerp, Belgium, and the 1924 Olympics in Paris. Costello repeated his winning ways at the 1928 Olympics in Amsterdam with a new partner, Charles McIlvaine. All of the races were won handily.

Source: http://en.wikipedia.org/wiki/Paul_Costello

This is a photo of the race from the 1916 national championship regatta in Duluth where Kent and Osman from the Duluth Boat Club handily beat the famed Vesper double of Kelly and Costello. In fairness to the Vesper duo, the Duluth team probably had a home course advantage because of the rough water, which is evident in the photo. Duluth rowers were used to rowing in rough water. Having a home crowd of several thousand madly cheering people probably helped as well.

NEMHC 52422 b5f2

INVINCIBLE: HISTORY OF THE DULUTH BOAT CLUB

The "Duluth giants," Art Osman (left) and Roy Kent (right) won the national championship in the senior double in 1915 and 1916, beating some very formidable competition from the Vesper Boat Club in Philadelphia.
NEMHC 52422 b5f2

Max Rheinberger Sr. proudly wears some of the medals that he won when he was part of the Invincible Four. The last medal that Rheinberger won in national competition was in the senior eight race of 1916. Rheinberger was one of the Duluth oarsmen who joined the service when the United States entered World War I; he served in Europe. From the private collection of the Rheinberger family.

each unit rowing, eating, and sleeping together, apart from the other units. At the end of the season, the boat club held a regatta in which the units raced against each other in all the various events. Medals and trophies were awarded to the victors. As it turned out, most of the races were won by the unit that trained under J. A. (young Jim) Ten Eyck.[37] The winners may have been the best oarsmen in America, but, of course, no such claim was made.

Inter-club competition was all that was held by the Duluth Boat Club in 1917, but in 1918, the Century Boat Club of Saint Louis, Missouri, came up to Duluth for a regatta. They seemed to be formidable opponents, being on the average over six feet tall and 190 pounds. Their record was as impressive as their physical stature, since they had won nineteen consecutive races. Training prevailed over size and strength, however, because the Century Boat Club lost every race to Duluth's youngsters.[38]

After the signing of the Armistice, the veteran oarsmen who returned from military service found that they could not win their seats in a boat from the young men that replaced them during their absence. The Duluth Boat Club's roster of oarsmen for 1919 read completely different from that of 1916.[39]

The change in personalities did not lead to a complete change of fortune, as the Duluth Boat Club convincingly dominated the National Regatta in Worcester, Massachusetts, in 1919. Duluth won the junior eight, intermediate double, intermediate four, intermediate eight, senior four, and senior eight.

CHAPTER 3: THE INVINCIBLE ERA

The Barnes Trophy was retained.[40] It may have seemed as though the Duluth Boat Club's reign of superiority would have no end.

Nineteen twenty was an Olympic year, and athletes all over the country were striving to be among those to represent the United States in Antwerp, Belgium, and those at the Duluth Boat Club were no exception. So far, the Duluthians had not really had an opportunity to make a bid for the Olympics. The 1916 Olympic games were cancelled because the world was at war, and 1912, the year of the last Olympic games to be held prior to 1920, was only the second year that the Duluth Boat Club had the coaching services of Ten Eyck, and they had not as yet developed their oarsmen to full potential.

The Duluth Boat Club oarsmen from 1920. UWS Dan Hill Library

A great deal of attention was focused on the senior eight race, because Syracuse and Navy, the two best college crews in the nation, had each won a race from the other by the slimmest of margins, and both crews were kept intact into the summer for an Olympic bid. The Duluth Boat Club, which had won every senior eight race since 1913, was also expected to make things interesting.

The year 1920 saw the closest senior eight race held in the U.S. Nationals since 1912, when Duluth lost the senior eight race to Winnipeg by one-quarter length. Duluth was equally unfortunate in 1920. Navy beat Syracuse by one-quarter length, with Duluth another one-half length behind. Duluth's bow lapped the stern of the winners, but it was only third place, nonetheless.[41] It was a double defeat for J. E. Ten Eyck, who coached the Syracuse crew and helped coach

The Duluth oarsmen started rowing at a young age, particularly during the First World War when men of age eligible to serve in the armed forces (eighteen and older) were not allowed to row for the DBC.

NEMHC 52422 b5f1

75

rowing stories

ALL OF THE FOLLOWING STORIES ARE FROM *THE ZENITH*, JULY 1916

DULUTH ROWING STYLE

The stroke that was taught by the elder Jim Ten Eyck at Syracuse had a short body swing with a high stroke rating. The shell maintains constant speed because the oars were hardly out of the water before there was a quick catch and power was jammed on for the next stroke. The younger Ten Eycks taught a long body swing, more in the English and Canadian style of the era. The hands were pulled in all the way to the body and there was a clean and quick recovery with fast hands and slow slide to avoid checking the boat.

THE BATTLE ROYAL IN PAJAMAS

The oarsmen occasionally mix a little humor with their arduous training. A few nights ago, the squad of 60 took the son of a prominent real estate and building manager and initiated him into their exclusive order of silent sleepers. They took him from his bed, pajama-clad, out onto the dock, [and] they soused him into the cold waters of the bay.

Some of the crowd stepped too near the edge to do the throwing and, like Daniel's furnace feeders, fell in themselves. Wishing for more company, there then ensued a battle royal on the float, which ended in the company needing a change and considerable roughdrying.

LINKIE, WHOSE YER FRIEND?

A drunken lumberjack, found on the street unprotected, was conveyed to the crew dormitory and put in the coxswain's bed. When the rightful tenant appeared and claimed his own, they say the argument that followed would bring down the house if reproduced in a talking machine and moving picture combination.

ROWING SHORT-HANDED

In a match inter-club race, held at Duluth a few years ago, the oar of an ex-Yale man sprung out of its socket, about three quarters of the way through the race. He was unable to latch it again, and his brother, an ex-Harvard man, commanded him to jump overboard. The Yale man was rowing No. 6, and as he stood up on his frail stretcher, to his full height of 6 feet 3 inches, and then dove over his brother's oar (No. 7), it made a sight that few observers are likely to forget.

The coxswain merely turned his head a fraction, called to the judge's launch to pick up his jettisoned oarsman, and then gave his full attention to stimulating the remaining three men left on the starboard side to increase their power, to lessen the drag on the rudder. Finishing—the short-handed crew lost by a very narrow margin but were quite proud of their accomplishment at that.

A DETONATOR

Jim Ten Eyck had a bowman in one of the early eights, of German descent, who never got warmed up until the race was about over. His fighting spirit never carried him up to high racing tension, until the crews were ready for their final sprint. So Jim decided that there must be some way of getting this Dutchman fighting mad, earlier in the game, if the boat was to get 100 percent from his efforts during the race.

Big Louis Thompson was stroke at that time, and as they were passing the quarter mile flag, Louis turned around and called back in the boat, "Boys, that — — — — of a Beschenbossel is laying down." B—'s answer was such that the fury of his efforts, at the bow, required all the strength that Thompson could muster on the other side to keep the shell from turning around. They won all rightee.

It was only when the race was over and "B" sought Thompson to whip him for the vile slander that the "job" was explained to him.

Duluth. Syracuse's victory over Navy for the 1920 Intercollegiate Rowing Association varsity eight championship was diminished.

Perhaps the Duluth Boat Club had some justifiable excuses that explained their defeat. The regatta was held early in the summer, rather than in August as was usual, so that the winners would have time to prepare for the Olympic games to be held later the same summer. This put the Duluth Boat Club at a distinct disadvantage because of the cold, northern climate. The Duluth oarsmen were usually a long way from peak condition in early summer and needed a few more months to develop speed. The college crews were racing in March, nearly two months before the ice went out of the Duluth-Superior harbor. The college oarsmen were near peak condition before the Duluth men started rowing. Had this race been held in August, the result might have been different. The Duluth Boat Club made no such excuse, however.

The young men in the Duluth senior eight of 1920 were quite young and relatively inexperienced. In 1920, the senior eight of the Duluth Boat Club was composed of men averaging 18¾ years of age, six in high school and the other two under 21.[42] Just the same, they gave a close race to the Navy eight, which went on to win gold medals at the Olympic games in Antwerp. The 1920 Navy crew has been judged to be among the all-time greatest college eights.[43]

The Duluth Boat Club fared little better in the rest of the 1920 National Regatta. The only event they won was the intermediate four. The Duluth Boat Club did get the satisfaction of accumulating enough second and third place points to be the aggregate champions, once again retaining the Barnes Trophy.[44]

In 1921, Duluth came back to dominate the national regatta once again. The Duluth Boat Club took firsts in the senior quad, senior four, and senior eight. Duluth also produced a single sculls champion for the first time in its history. Walter M. Hoover won the senior association single, the senior quarter-mile dash single, and the championship single. Duluth easily won the Barnes Trophy.[45]

DBC National Champions 1921. From the right are Spielmacher (bow), F. Champion, A. Haug, B. Vincent, H. Quade, J. Woods, R. Erickson, F. Bridgeman (stroke), and Mitchell (coxswain).

Photo from David Bjorkman personal collection

The Diamond Sculls, which is the award given to the champion sculler at the Royal British Henley Regatta at Henley-on-Thames in England, was regarded as symbolic of world supremacy in sculling and one of the most honored awards in sporting. John B. Kelly, American sculling champion, was denied a chance to compete at Henley because the Henley stewards ruled that only gentlemen were eligible, and Kelly did not fit their definition of gentlemen since he had done manual labor during his life. As a result, outraged Americans tried to institute an award of their own to be symbolic of world championship, a title that they thought Kelly deserved. With this in mind, the Philadelphia Gold Challenge Cup was founded, and Jack Kelly won it, as everyone expected. Kelly then went on to win two gold medals in the 1920 Olympic games in the single and in the double sculls with his cousin Paul Costello. Kelly retired as

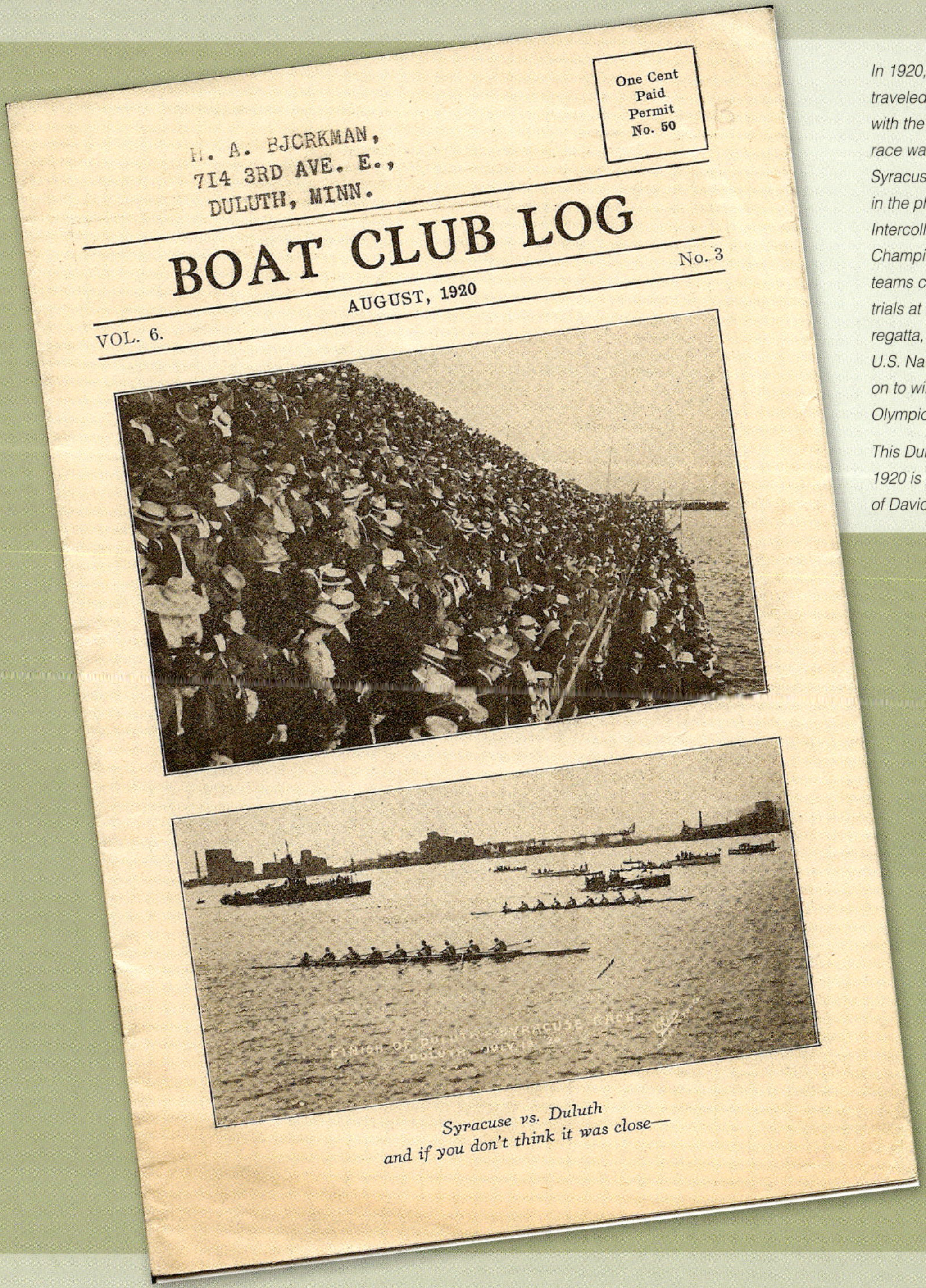

H. A. BJORKMAN,
714 3RD AVE. E.,
DULUTH, MINN.

One Cent
Paid
Permit
No. 50

BOAT CLUB LOG

VOL. 6.   AUGUST, 1920   No. 3

Syracuse vs. Duluth
and if you don't think it was close—

In 1920, the University of Syracuse traveled to Duluth for a dual match with the Duluth Boat Club. The eight race was almost a dead heat with Syracuse winning by inches as shown in the photo. Syracuse had won the Intercollegiate Rowing Association Championship in 1920. Both of these teams competed in the 1920 Olympic trials at the National Championship regatta, but lost in a close race to the U.S. Naval Academy crew that went on to win the gold medal in the 1920 Olympics.

This Duluth Boat Club log from August 1920 is part of the personal collection of David Bjorkman.

The Philadelphia Gold Challenge Cup was a traveling trophy to be awarded to the reigning champion single sculler of the world. When Walter Hoover won this honor in 1922, he received a presentation award to keep. This photo actually shows an exact replica of the original award (permanently lost by theft), which was presented to Walter Hoover by the oarsmen of the Detroit Boat Club who he coached to Olympic success in the 1950s.

Photo provided by Walter Hoover Jr.

champion and gave the Gold Cup to Costello to defend against all contenders. Walter Hoover easily won this cup in June 1922.[46] Hoover's sculling accomplishments eventually made him an international superstar.

Since the Gold Challenge Cup was recognized as symbolic of world championship only in America, Hoover tried to cement his claim to the title by applying to row for the Diamond Sculls at the Royal Henley Regatta the same year. The Henley stewards found Hoover to be acceptable since he was a civil engineer by profession and had not ever been employed at manual labor.

For his Henley attempt, Hoover made the careful preparation that was characteristic of Duluth Boat Club endeavors. Hoover was in Henley, England, two weeks prior to the regatta, rowing on the Thames, getting well acquainted with the course. The Duluthian astonished English observers by bringing several barrels of Lake Superior water with him for drinking purposes.[47] It was evident to all who came in contact with Hoover that he was completely ready for his races in 1922.

The Henley Regatta of 1922 was the stormiest in history. Hoover won his first heat against R. J. C. Tweed, an English college student, rowing in the remnants of a gale that had swept the Henley course. He rowed slowly and carefully through the rough water to win with a time of 10:41, which was good for the conditions. The second heat matched Hoover against A. Bayne, an Australian sculler who was undefeated. Hoover beat Bayne by three lengths in a heavy rainstorm.[48]

Walter Hoover shown posing in his single racing shell, which he designed.

Photo provided by Walter Hoover Jr.

In the final, Hoover faced Jack Beresford Jr., winner of the Diamond Sculls in 1920 and winner of the silver medal in the single sculls in the 1920 Olympics. The race was rowed on July 8, which had weather that was much like that of the preceding days. They managed to hold the event between rainsqualls, but the scullers had to row into a strong wind.

Photograph of the Royal Henley Regatta held in Henley, England. Contestants raced two at a time over this somewhat narrow course. A series of elimination heats determined who would meet in the finals.

From a postcard in the author collection

Walter Hoover on the right shaking hands with Jack Beresford after defeating him in the 1922 Diamond Sculls at the Royal Henley Regatta.

Walter Hoover in his single after winning the Diamond Sculls in 1922.

Photo provided by Walter Hoover Jr.

JACK BERESFORD

DEFEATED BY WALTER HOOVER FOR THE DIAMOND SCULLS AT THE ROYAL HENLEY REGATTA IN 1922

Jack Beresford won rowing medals in five straight Olympics. From http://en.wikipedia.org/wiki/Jack_Beresford

Jack Beresford was one of the most accomplished rowers of his generation. He won medals at five straight Olympics. Beresford would have been a favorite for a medal in the 1940 Olympics in the double scull event, but those games were cancelled because of World War II.

Beresford won a silver medal at the 1920 Olympics in Antwerp in the single scull and a gold medal in the single scull in the 1924 Olympics in Paris. In 1928, he won a silver medal rowing in the eight at the Olympics in Amsterdam. He won a gold medal in the coxless four at the Los Angeles Olympics in 1928. In 1936, he won a gold medal in the double scull at the Olympics in Berlin. Beresford was the flag bearer for the British delegation at the opening ceremonies in 1936. He said that the double race in Berlin was the "sweetest race" he ever rowed. Beresford and his partner in the double, L. F. (Dick) Southwood, came from a length down to pass the favored Germans in the final two hundred meters, with Adolph Hitler watching.

Beresford won the Diamond Sculls at the Henley Royal Regatta in 1920, 1924, 1925, and 1926; the Silver Goblets & Nickalls Challenge Cup (pair) in 1928 and 1929; the Stewards Challenge Cup (coxless four) in 1932; and the Grand Challenge Cup (eight) in 1923 and 1928. In 1922, he lost the finals of the Diamond Sculls to Walter Hoover from the Duluth Boat Club.

Between 1920 and 1927, Beresford won the Wingfield Sculls, for the Amateur Sculling Championship of the Thames and Great Britain, for eight consecutive years, a streak unmatched in history.

With his win in the single scull at the 1924 Olympic Games came the Philadelphia Gold Cup, awarded by the Schuylkill Navy for the amateur sculling championship of the world. He successfully defended the Cup against Walter Hoover in 1925 before indicating to its stewards that he no longer wished to contest it.

During the First World War, Beresford was wounded in France. He returned to London and learned the craft of making furniture in his father's factory.

His contribution to rowing was recognized with two honors in the 1940s: the gold medal of the International Rowing Federation (1947), and the Olympic diploma of merit (1949). In 1960, Beresford was appointed a Commander of the British Empire. In 2005, a Blue Plaque was erected by English Heritage at Beresford's home from 1903 to 1940, 19 Grove Park Gardens in Chiswick, West London. Beresford is one of the first sportsmen to receive this honor.

Source: http://en.wikipedia.org/wiki/Jack_Beresford

Hoover immediately took the lead from Beresford at the start and increased it all the way to win by almost fifty yards, one of the largest margins of victory ever seen in a Diamond Sculls final.[49]

Upon winning this race, Walter Hoover became a world-famous athletic figure. The British were very impressed with the power and grace of the Duluth sculler, and there was much speculation that Hoover would have been capable of setting a new record at Henley had the weather conditions been less adverse. Hoover was only the second American ever to win the Diamond Sculls; Edward Hanlon Ten Eyck was the first. Consequently, Americans who were residing or visiting in England jubilantly displayed blue-and-white banners bearing Hoover's name.[50]

The news of Hoover's Henley success was received with tremendous excitement in the United States. The *New York Times* printed several articles concerning Hoover, one of which discussed the peculiarities of his style of rowing:

> *Walter Hoover, the Duluth sculling marvel, whose phenomenal rise has attracted international attention, achieved his coveted position by virtue of a particular style of rowing which aspirants to his title may have considerable difficulty in mastering.[51]*

Of course, the people most excited were Hoover's fellow Duluthians. Many people in Duluth were thrilled that their city was made known to the world by this Henley victory. Upon learning of Hoover's victory, the *Duluth News Tribune* sought to record the reactions of the populace. Some of the various comments follow:

> *Never before have we had the name of Duluth so suddenly and widely made famous as now. It has been broadcasted over every available part of the world. It has been thrust into the mouths of millions . . . Duluth is fixed in the minds of people, as it never was before. Maps have been marked, and our population ascertained and our resources have surprised many, while our natural harbor and wonderful commercial advantages are known and common talk the world over.[52]*

> *Hoover's victory will put Duluth on the map, not only in sports, but will give this city wonderful publicity.[53]*

> *Walter Hoover . . . has done more to bring fame to Duluth than any other individual in the city.[54]*

Some people gave credit to Julius Barnes for his part in this, as well as other Duluth Boat Club rowing victories.

> *From its first small initial club victory to its large rowing institution of the present day, the most prominent in the United States and the world, is in a large measure due to a fellow citizen, Julius H. Barnes. He has given unreservedly. When citizens are asked to support the club, they are getting more than dollar for dollar value and the city gets more advertising in every other branch.[55]*

> *But for his [Barnes] years of generous encouragement and support of the Duluth Boat Club, this town would not possess its worldwide reputation in aquatics, and the name Duluth would not be known from pole to pole.[56]*

Duluthians immediately made elaborate preparations for an enormous welcome home celebration for Hoover. A special committee was formed to plan this celebration. Every day, during the three weeks it took Hoover to get back from England, the *Duluth News Tribune* ran articles that beseeched its readers to mail in any suggestions that they might have for the celebration, and any ideas that were proposed were printed. One person thought that the city should erect an enormous statue of Walter Hoover sitting in his boat.[57] The *Duluth News Tribune* published a large photograph of Hoover, as a supplement to their paper, and they advocated that everyone in Duluth have this picture in the window of their home to welcome Hoover back.[58] To finance the festivities, Walter Hoover buttons were sold for one dollar apiece.[59] While Hoover's fellow Duluthians were readying their welcome for him, he received a vigorous reception in New York when he arrived there. According to the *Duluth News Tribune*'s special correspondent, Hoover was greeted by a flotilla of boats carrying a score of welcoming committees and several bands, which were playing

CHAPTER 3: THE INVINCIBLE ERA

in his honor. He was saluted by the guns of a flagship, and upon disembarking, Hoover was escorted to New York's city hall, where he was formally received by city dignitaries.[60] The *New York Times* also reported that Hoover received an enthusiastic greeting in their city.[61]

The celebration of Hoover's homecoming to Duluth was worthy of the elaborate plans that were made. When Hoover arrived on the train, thousands of people were at the depot to greet him. After several speeches, Hoover was placed at the head of a large parade that moved through the city. All of the various organizations in town participated: the Veterans, Lions, Elks, American Legion, fire department, police department, engineers' club, etc. There were bands, drum and bugle corps, and several floats. Wreaths, bunting, draping, and flags hung from buildings on Superior and First Street. Later in the evening, a large festival was held in the streets of downtown Duluth. It was estimated that there were 65,000 people in attendance (there were fewer than 100,000 people living in Duluth at this time). This was the largest gathering of people that has ever taken place for any reason in the city of Duluth. The open merry-making and dancing in the streets lasted through the night into the morning hours.[62] The *Duluth News Tribune* also reported that a subscription was raised by the citizens of Duluth to provide Walter Hoover and his wife a furnished home as a token of their esteem. However, Walter Hoover stated in his memoir that the Duluth Boat Club stepped in and claimed the lion's share of the $5,300 raised for expenses. Hoover was able to keep $1,700, which he spent on a new Cole Roadster.[63]

Photographs from the Duluth News Tribune *show Walter Hoover welcomed home to Duluth after winning the Diamond Sculls and Philadelphia Gold Challenge. Hoover's homecoming was probably the largest gathering of people in Duluth's history.*

Newspaper clippings from the David Bjorkman personal collection

In 1923, Hoover tried to retain his Diamond Sculls title at the Royal Henley Regatta, but lost. This was the last year that Hoover competed for the Duluth Boat Club, but he went on to lead a very colorful and eventful life both in and out of rowing.

Walter Hoover's Henley victory overshadowed some other remarkable rowing performances in 1922 by Duluth Boat Club oarsmen that deserved more attention than they received. While attention centered on Hoover, the rest of the Duluth Boat Club's oarsmen were nearly forgotten since it was thought that they were not as fast as previous Duluth crews. The newspaper expressed unusual pessimism over the chances of the sweep oarsmen. Before the North-Western Regatta, the boat club officers were led to state that unless the Duluth crews made a respectable showing in the North-Western, they would not be entered in the National Regatta in Philadelphia.[64]

WALTER HOOVER
WORLD CHAMPION SCULLER

Walter Hoover, World Champion. Photo provided by Walter Hoover Jr.

Walter Hoover began rowing for the Duluth Boat Club in 1913 at the age of eighteen. That same year, he was a member of the junior eight that finished first at the North-Western International Rowing Association (NWIRA) regatta in Saint Paul. Hoover and his teammates went on to win the intermediate eight at the U.S. National Championships in Boston and beat their own senior eight from Duluth in the senior eight finals.

In 1914, Hoover took up sculling and won the junior and senior single event at the NWIRA regatta in Kenora, Ontario. He also rowed in the winning senior eight at the national championships in Philadelphia in 1914.

The next year, Hoover again won the senior single at the 1915 NWIRA in Winnipeg, along with the single quarter-mile dash. At the 1915 Nationals in Springfield, Massachusetts, Hoover lost a turning race to Waldo Smith. Hoover claimed that Smith's turning buoy had drifted downstream 125 feet, giving him an advantage of several lengths. The race was protested, but the officials denied the request for a re-run. Hoover did win the quarter-mile dash at the Nationals in a time of 1:08. He entered the Labor Day Regatta in Philadelphia to race the great Jack Kelly. Hoover and Kelly had a very tight race, with Hoover coming from behind to take the lead near the finish line when he caught a crab, blacked out, and stopped dead.

Nineteen sixteen promised to be a big year for Hoover, with the U.S. National Championships being held in Duluth. However, history had other plans. Hoover was a private in the Third Minnesota Infantry National Guard, which was called up to chase the bandit Pancho Villa down on the Mexican border. The military was also part of Hoover's life in 1917 when he was drafted into the army and served as a second lieutenant in the Thirty-third artillery.

When Hoover returned to Duluth, he found his sculling so unsatisfactory that he nearly quit. Instead, he planned out a program that was designed to make him a champion. Hoover did three miles of roadwork daily to strengthen his legs and develop his cardiovascular system. He even ran in snow during the winter. Hoover followed a strict diet like other Duluth oarsmen, but most importantly, he put in long hours sculling. Hoover developed his technique, speed, and rowing form in the Duluth harbor, and he learned seamanship in the choppy waves and strong winds of open Lake Superior.

In 1920, Hoover did not compete, but while he was working for the International Paper Company in International Falls designing insulate plants, he designed a racing shell that he would use later to win the world championship. Hoover was a civil engineer by profession, and he used his technical knowledge to design his own shell along the lines of a naval torpedo. His shell was considered rather unorthodox because Hoover had his seat lower in the boat than other scullers, which gave him a lower center of gravity.

Besides planning his own training program and designing his own shell, Hoover also developed a unique sculling style. He did a short stroke with a rapid arm movement at an extremely high rating. Observers have noted that Hoover had extremely muscular arms and that he used them in his sculling more than other competent scullers used theirs. Hoover's style, shell, and training were designed for his own personal characteristics. Because Hoover disregarded common wisdom, nearly everything about him was considered unorthodox.

At the 1921 National Championships in Buffalo, Hoover gained national renown by winning the intermediate single, senior single, and the quarter-mile dash.

Hoover also won the senior single and the single dash events at the Peoples Regatta in Philadelphia on July 4, 1921. Photo of trophies from the St. Louis County Historical Society by Bruce Ojard Photographics

Walter Hoover was so popular after winning the Diamond Sculls that a song was composed in his honor.

Image of Hoover sheet music obtained from the Friends of Rowing History website http://www.rowinghistory.net/

In 1922, the race for the Philadelphia Gold Challenge Cup was held early in May, and because of typical spring weather conditions in Duluth, Hoover only had three weeks on the water to train for the event. Still, Hoover easily beat Paul Costello by over two lengths of open water and beat Jack Kelly's course record by eleven seconds. Julius Barnes hastily arranged a passport for Hoover, and he sailed the next day on the *Mauritania* for England to compete for the Diamond Sculls at the Henley-on-Thames Royal Regatta. Hoover easily won his two heats, including a victory over A. Baynes, the undefeated Australian sculling champion. In the finals, Hoover beat the famous English sculler, Jack Beresford, by a huge margin of 29.8 seconds. This was the first time in twenty-five years that an American had won the Diamond Sculls, and Hoover immediately became world famous. When he returned to New York, there was an enormous welcome at the docks and a ticker-tape parade up Broadway. When Hoover finally got back to Duluth, the celebration in his honor was the largest party in the city's history, including up to the present day.

Hoover made two more attempts to win the Diamond Sculls. In 1923, Hoover returned to Henley as a strong favorite, but he was beaten as a result of peculiar circumstances. Hoover was racing in a heat against D. H. L. Gollan of Leander, a deaf mute and an excellent sculler. In 1923, the Henley course was narrowed from ninety to seventy-five feet. Right at the start, a freak crosswind pushed the bow of Hoover's shell against the wooden booms that lined the sides of the course. Gollan passed Hoover, as the latter struck his port blade against these booms. In a hasty attempt to catch Gollan, Hoover once again struck his oar blade against the booms, this time breaking a chunk out of the blade. Although these initial problems gave Gollan a lead of nearly ten lengths, Hoover never gave up and sculled so smoothly and powerfully for the remainder of the race that he finished less than a length behind Gollan. The spectators, astonished at the magnificent finish, gave an excited burst of applause when Hoover, grinning, paddled over to Gollan and shook his hand.

The British were very impressed with this showmanship of Hoover's, and he gained popularity by his response to suggestions that he would have won had he been less unfortunate. Hoover said, "It was my business to steer my shell as well as shove it through the water. Gollan won, so all credit goes to him."

In 1925, Hoover made another attempt at winning the Diamond Sculls, but this time lost to Jack Beresford, who used a boat of Hoover's design and who hired Hoover's former boatman. During 1926, Hoover rowed and

This postcard of Walter Hoover shows him holding his awards after winning the Diamond Sculls.

From the personal collection of Joseph Kormann

was head coach at the Undine Barge Club in Philadelphia, where his rowers won forty-three races in the course of the year. During this year, Hoover also designed the first single to have moving shoes and outriggers and designed another boat that was built with a hull made with an aluminum alloy. Among other races, Hoover won the championship single, double, and single dash at the Canadian Henley Regatta in St. Catherines, Ontario.

Hoover didn't row in 1927, but in 1928 he tried a comeback for the Olympics. He was beaten in the trials by Ken Meyers but made the team as an alternate in the single. Hoover was thirty-three years old and in his own judgment "well past his prime." After 1928, he retired as a competitive rower.

Hoover later moved to Detroit, where he coached rowers from the Detroit Boat Club. In 1956, Hoover entered his eight oarsmen from the Detroit Boat Club in all events at the Olympic trials. Their eight-man crew included men who rowed in the four, the double, the single, and one lightweight who was only in the eight. Yale beat the eight by a length. Hoover's Detroit oarsmen won the straight four and double events, and both crews went on to win silver medals at the Olympics in Melbourne, Australia. Yale went on to win the Olympic gold in the eight.

After Detroit, Hoover moved to Lone Pine, California, where he spent years prospecting for gold as a mining engineer. He was away from rowing until 1978 when he coached the Minneapolis Rowing Club. In 1979, Hoover was the women's crew coach at Kansas State University. Nineteen eighty-two saw Hoover working on the design of new rowing shells, including a single with moving shoes and outriggers (prior to this design being barred from international competition). Walter Hoover died in 1984 at the age of eighty-nine.

In 1921, Walter Hoover won both the Senior Single and the Senior Single Quarter Mile Dash at the National Championship Regatta in Buffalo, New York. This banner is in the St. Louis County Historical Society collection.

Photograph by Bruce Ojard Photographics

It seemed to be a surprise when the Duluth Boat Club won the North-Western Regatta easily over favored Winnipeg in 1922. Consequently, sixteen men were chosen to go to Philadelphia to represent the club. Hoover was the only respectable sculler in the club, and he declined to risk his title at the Nationals since he had not rowed for a month following the Henley Regatta. So, only sweep events were entered by Duluth. In the past, the Duluth Boat Club usually sent at least thirty men to the Nationals, so this contingent was smaller than usual.

Nineteen twenty-two was the fiftieth anniversary of the founding of the National Association of Amateur Oarsmen, so the regatta held that year was celebrated as a Golden Jubilee Regatta. Perhaps this was one reason why there were more entries from more rowing organizations than ever before. Another reason may be that the location of the regatta on the Schuylkill River in Philadelphia was the heart of the rowing world. All together, thirty-three different clubs had entries. Because of the amount and quality of competition, no one club was expected to dominate the Nationals in 1922. The Duluth Boat Club, with only sixteen oarsmen entered in only five events, was not thought to have much chance of winning the Barnes Trophy again.

During the first day of competition, Duluth won the intermediate eight and four. One hour after the intermediate four race, the same oarsmen entered the senior international four race, which they nearly won, in spite of being quite tired from the first race. They lost the senior international four race by only four feet to a crack crew from the Vesper Boat Club of Philadelphia.[65] On the final day of competition, Duluth won the remaining two races they had entered, the senior four and the senior eight. It was a surprise to most people that the Duluth Boat Club not only retained the Barnes Trophy in 1922, but they won it with a comfortable margin of points.

Gold medals won by Dr. William Coventry while rowing for Duluth. In 1922, Coventry won national championships in the intermediate four and senior four. His crew also took second in the international senior four, losing to the Vesper Boat Club of Philadelphia by a scant four feet after fighting hard to come back from being a length and a half down at the halfway point. This race was rowed only an hour and a half after their victory in the intermediate four. Coventry's crewmates were Letourneau, Ward, and Dever. Photo by the author of medals belonging to Mrs. William Coventry

On January 2, 1923, the *Christian Science Monitor* scooped the local newspapers in announcing:

> For the first time in 12 years, the rowing crews of the Duluth Boat Club next season will not be coached by a Ten Eyck. Members of the rowing committee of the local organization, after discussion and consideration lasting several weeks, have at last come to a decision to institute a professional policy which has been in vogue for more than a decade . . .
>
> An experiment has been tried here for three years, starting the early season workouts under the guidance of one of the former oarsmen, and permitting the finishing touches to be applied by the elder Ten Eyck when he arrived

here from the east about July 1, or shortly thereafter. But this has resulted in the younger coach doing about 4/5 of the work and getting about 1/5 of the credit.[66]

In explaining the reasons behind this action, the boat club officers indicated that there was to be a shifting of values. The fame and glory of winning races were not as important as the personal good that an oarsman could get from participating in the Duluth Boat Club program. Professional coaching was considered unnecessary. Money was also admitted to be a factor in their decision.[67]

The idealistic reasons that the officers of the Duluth Boat Club gave for their decision were valid, but the major reason was left unmentioned. Julius Barnes, who had paid all of the boat club's rowing expenses himself, had tried to get other members of the Duluth Boat Club to make contributions to the rowing program. However, Duluthians were content to let Barnes remain the sole benefactor of Duluth rowing. Barnes finally reached the conclusion that his continued sole contribution demonstrated that the club members and citizens of Duluth were not interested enough to support rowing with money of their own, and if they were uninterested, then his contributions seemed rather meaningless. Barnes, therefore, decided that the Duluth Boat Club and its rowing program would have to sink or swim on its own.

The Ten Eycks left the Duluth Boat Club with a record of nearly unbroken success. During the thirty years of rowing previous to 1911 and the hiring of J. A. Ten Eyck as coach by Barnes, the Duluth Boat Club had won less than half a dozen races, all junior events in the North-Western association. As far as rowing was concerned, the Duluth

The photo is undated, but this is the Duluth Senior Eight from 1923. They lost the National Championship Senior Eight Race in 1923 to the Undine Barge Club of Philadelphia in a race so close it was disputed. The rowers and spectators thought that the DBC came from behind to row through Undine with a furious sprint at the finish to win, but the finish line officials decided otherwise. The men shown won several national championships in the 1920s. The individuals in the photograph from top left are Tinkham, Coventry, Quade, Hector, Champion, and Brown. At the bottom are Vincent, Bjorkman, Homerud, and Markham. NEMHC 52422 b5f2

Boat Club was unknown outside of Minnesota and western Ontario. Under the coaching of the three Ten Eycks, the Duluth Boat Club dominated the North-Western Rowing Association every year, with the exception of 1911 and 1920. Duluth won forty-three national championship races and won the grand aggregate championship, represented by the Barnes Trophy, five times and would have won it three other years, except that it had not yet been instituted. The Duluth Boat Club, at one time, held the record time for every event in the National Regatta. Some of the records are still unsurpassed and probably never will be, since the racing distance has since been shortened from 1.25 miles to 2,000 meters.

Duluth's rowing success did not cease immediately in the absence of the Ten Eycks. In 1923, the Duluth Boat Club made a strong enough showing at the National Regatta in Baltimore to win the Barnes Trophy once again. Duluth won the intermediate single, intermediate double, and senior quad. The senior eight race was lost to the Undine Boat Club of Philadelphia in a race that was so close that the finish was officially protested.[68] Most spectators thought that Duluth had won by a quarter length.

Nineteen twenty-three was the last year that the Duluth Boat Club made a big showing in the National Regatta. In 1924, there was no competitive rowing at the Duluth Boat Club. In 1925, the Duluth Boat Club entered the National Regatta again, winning the intermediate eight race and losing the senior eight race to the Undine Barge Club of Philadelphia once again, by three seconds.[69] This was the last year that the Duluth Boat Club sent oarsmen to the Nationals. The club dissolved in 1926.

In assessing the factors responsible for the rowing success of the Duluth Boat Club—the tremendous athletes, the training program, the coaching of the Ten Eycks, the excellent equipment, the superb rowing and training facilities, and the idealism of the club—they have one common denominator, Julius H. Barnes. Recognition has to go to the oarsmen for their individual endeavors, but there was not one single oarsman, including Walter Hoover, who played as important a part in the Duluth Boat Club's rowing record as Barnes.

Trophies in the Duluth Boat Club collection of the St. Louis County Historical Society. Photo by Bruce Ojard Photographics

One of the many banners won by the Invincible Four. Photo of artifacts from the St. Louis County Historical Society by Bruce Ojard Photographics

Some of the banners won by the Duluth Boat Club.

Photos of artifacts from the St. Louis County Historical Society by Bruce Ojard Photographics

CHAPTER 3: THE INVINCIBLE ERA

1. *Duluth News Tribune*, July 30, 1896, p. 1.
2. Karl Twedt, Program of the Northwestern International Rowing Association, 1970, St. Paul, MN.
3. Ibid.
4. *Duluth News Tribune*, July 15, 1906, sec. 4, p. 1.
5. Twedt, op. cit.
6. DBC Yearbook, 1908, Huntley Publishing Co., Duluth Boat Club records, NEMHC S3009.
7. *Duluth News Tribune*, July 22, 1911, p. 1.
8. *Duluth News Tribune*, July 30, 1911, Sporting sec., p. 1.
9. *Duluth News Tribune*, August 13, 1912, p. 6.
10. *Boston Daily Globe*, August 10, 1913, p. 1.
11. Walter F. Dunn, *Public Ledger-Philadelphia*, August 10, 1914, Sporting sec., p. 1.
12. *New York Times*, August 16, 1915, Sport sec., p. 2.
13. Ibid.
14. Interview with Henning E. Peterson.
15. Robert A. Dahl, "Rowing as Duluth Does It, A Club That Has Won 56 Firsts in Six Years-And The Reasons Why," *Outing*, September 1918, p. 371.
16. *Springfield Daily Republic*, August 14, 1915, p. 1.
17. Duluth Herald, n.d. (circa 1914), A. R. Kent Scrapbook, Duluth Boat Club records, NEMHC S3009.
18. *Springfield Daily Republic*, August 14, 1915, p. 1.
19. Memo, n.d., J. D. Mahoney Scrapbook, Duluth Boat Club records, NEMHC S3009.
20. Interview with Henning E. Peterson.
21. Gil Fawcett, TV Script, KDAL-TV, May 4, 1949.
22. Dr. William F. Coventry, "An Oarsman's Reminiscences," unpublished memoir, n.d. (circa 1970s).
23. Duluth Oarsman's Diet, Duluth Boat Club records, NEMHC S3009.
24. Coventry, op. cit.
25. Interview with Henning E. Peterson.
26. Dahl, op. cit., p. 373.
27. Interview with Henning E. Peterson.
28. DBC Main Café payroll sheet, August 1916, J. D. Mahoney Scrapbook, Duluth Boat Club records, NEMHC S3009.
29. DBC Main Café Menu, June 15, 1912, J. D. Mahoney Scrapbook, Duluth Boat Club records, NEMHC S3009.
30. Dunn, loc. cit.
31. *Duluth News Tribune*, April 25, 1916, p. 10.
32. Alison McBean Buckingham interview, n.d., NEMHC S2250 tape 28.
33. Ibid.
34. *Duluth News Tribune*, August 14, 1916, p. 4.
35. Ibid.
36. *Duluth News Tribune*, August 12, 1916, p. 1.
37. Interview with Henning E. Peterson.
38. Ibid.
39. *Christian Science Monitor*, January 2, 1923.
40. *New York Tribune*, August 3, 1919, p. 17.
41. Boat Club Log, August 1920, vol. 6, no. 3, p. 4, Duluth Boat Club records, NEMHC S3009.
42. *Christian Science Monitor*, January 2, 1923.
43. *NAAO Rowing Guide* (National Association of Amateur Oarsmen), Philadelphia, 1968, p. 114.
44. Ibid.
45. Ibid.
46. Robert Kelley, *American Rowing, Its Background and Traditions* (G. P. Putnam's Sons, New York, London, 1932), p. 191.
47. *Duluth News Tribune*, July 9, 1922, p. 7.
48. Kelley, op. cit., p. 191.
49. *Times* (London), July 10, 1922, p. 5.
50. *Duluth News Tribune*, July 10, 1922, p. 7.
51. *New York Times*, August 6, 1922, p. 26.
52. *Duluth News Tribune*, July 13, 1922, p. 8.
53. *Duluth News Tribune*, July 9, 1922, p. 1.
54. Ibid.
55. *Duluth News Tribune*, July 13, 1922, editorial p. 7.
56. *Duluth News Tribune*, July 8, 1922, p. 1.
57. *Duluth News Tribune*, July 8, 1922, p. 1.
58. *Duluth News Tribune*, July 23, 1922, p. 1.
59. *Duluth News Tribune*, July 26, 1922, p. 1.
60. Ibid.
61. *New York Times*, July 26, 1922, p. 9.
62. *Duluth News Tribune*, July 29, 1922, p. 1.
63. Unpublished, undated memoir by Walter Hoover Sr., copy in author's collection.
64. *Duluth News Tribune*, August 3, 1922, p. 18.
65. *New York Times*, August 26, 1922, p. 18.
66. *Christian Science Monitor*, January 2, 1923, clipping from DBC file, NEMHC.
67. Ibid.
68. *Baltimore Sun*, August 5, 1923, p. 15.
69. *Duluth News Tribune*, August 9, 1925, p. 7.w

*NEMHC refers to the Northeast Minnesota Historical Center, archives of the St. Louis County Historical Society.

CHAPTER 4

decline and fall

The decline of the Duluth Boat Club began thirteen years before it finally collapsed in 1926. From a membership peak of 1,400 in 1912, the club decreased to 800 members in 1915.[1] Even with 800 members, the Duluth Boat Club was still easily the largest water-oriented club in America, but the decline, nonetheless, had serious consequences. The operating expenses of the boat club were funded entirely from membership fees and dues, with the exception of the rowing expenses, which were paid by Julius Barnes personally. By 1909, the physical plant of the boat club had expanded to the point where a huge membership was necessary for its upkeep. A decline in membership became dangerous to the existence of the organization.

One of the reasons for the decline of the Duluth Boat Club was apparent while the decline was taking place. The automobile became the center of activity for those who could afford one, and the boat club was composed of people who had the necessary wealth. Formerly, people who lived in Duluth were forced to seek their recreation within the city boundaries unless they wanted to take on an expedition. With the evolvement of the automobile from a novelty to a convenient form of transportation and with the construction of adequate roads, recreation could be sought elsewhere. Not only did recreation outside the city boundaries become accessible, but it also became preferable, since the auto was regarded as a source as well as a means of enjoyment. People looked for excuses to drive their cars. The lake country north of Duluth opened up, and people purchased summer homes on lakes that they could drive to. Naturally, people began to have less need for what the boat club offered.

The original aerial bridge was not actually a bridge but a structure with a large gondola that carried people and vehicles across the ship canal separating Park Point from the mainland of Duluth.

Postcard image provided by Jerry Paulson http://www.duluth-mn-usa.com/

This is a close-up of the gondola that carried the vehicles and passengers across the canal to Park Point.

Postcard image provided by Jerry Paulson http://www.duluth-mn-usa.com/

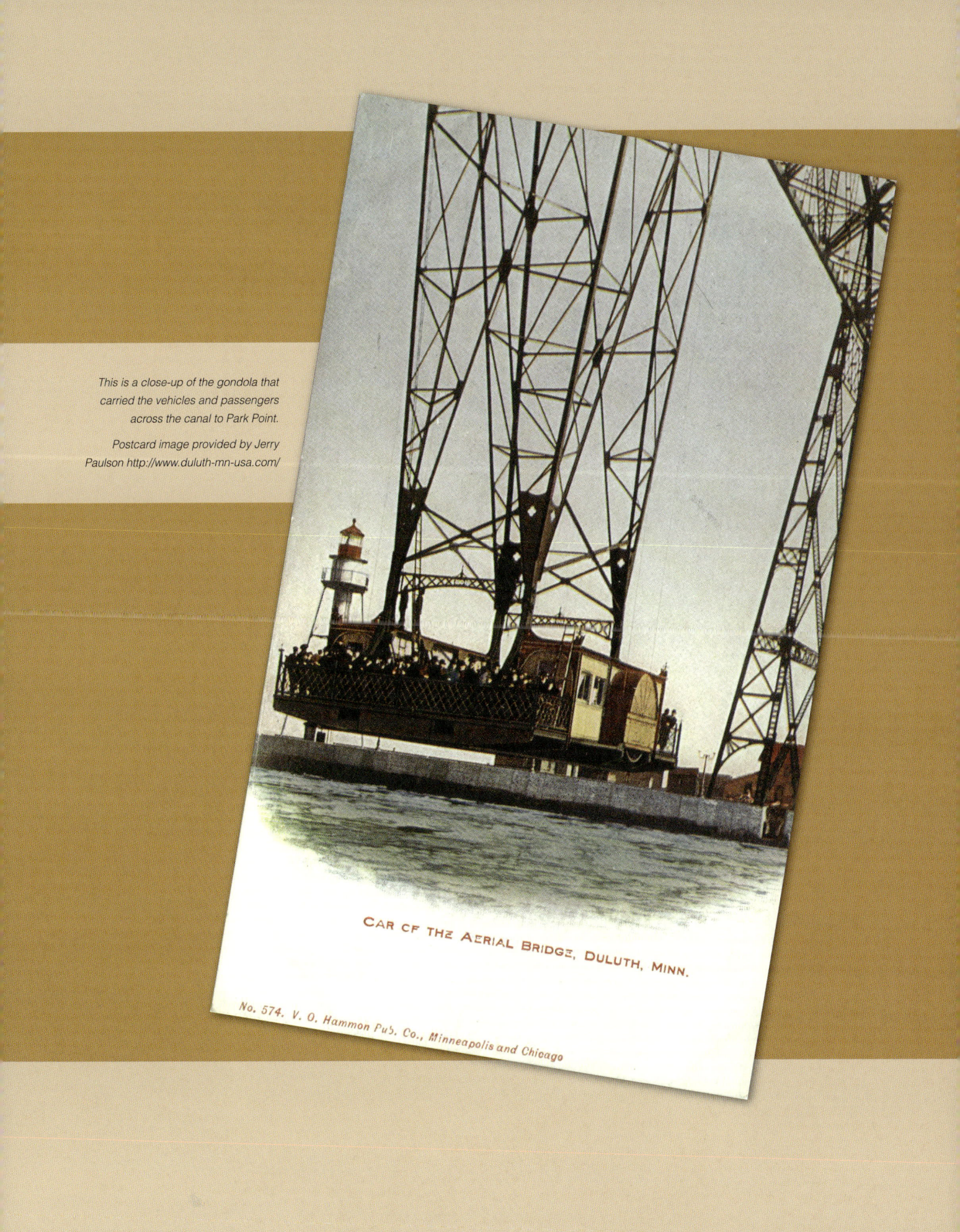

CAR OF THE AERIAL BRIDGE, DULUTH, MINN.

No. 574. V. O. Hammon Pub. Co., Minneapolis and Chicago

INVINCIBLE: HISTORY OF THE DULUTH BOAT CLUB

The boat club had been a very accessible place and close to the business area of the city. This changed once people stopped using public transportation in favor of their automobiles. For car owners, the boat club was not a convenient place to go to because the aerial bridge could only handle eight cars in one trip. So the canal that separated Minnesota Point from the mainland became a bottleneck. Cars going to and from the boat club were often jammed up in large numbers on both sides of the canal. This was especially true when large events, such as water carnivals, were taking place. There would have been no problem had people been willing to continue using the streetcar, but people preferred to just stay away from the boat club and go someplace where automobile travel was more convenient.

Despite their realization that the automobile was the boat club's nemesis, the officers of the Duluth Boat Club were surprised and annoyed that the Duluth Boat Club was losing support since it continued to offer an array of social and recreational activity. Julius Barnes expressed this disappointment in an open letter to boat club members in 1916:

> *Owing to various causes, perhaps among others the replacement by the automobile of the motorboats, the club membership has declined until it is no longer self-sustaining, even though the club has always been relieved of the direct expenses of rowing entirely. Is there not local pride enough in the organization to maintain a membership list in this city of 100,000 that can keep this club paying its way? Does it not furnish enough amusement and entertainment for people of all ages to justify its scale of dues?*[2]

The decline of the boat club was not constant. To make their club suitable for the National Regatta of 1916, a huge membership drive was undertaken, which succeeded in raising the number of members to 1,262.[3] To gain as many members as they did, the boat club lowered the initiation fee from thirty dollars to ten dollars.[4]

The National Regatta of 1916 did, in fact, rejuvenate enthusiasm in the boat club. Julius Barnes tried to make this renewed interest permanent by donating the natatorium to the Duluth Boat Club. This did become a definite attraction, but it was not enough to keep the necessary large membership. Actually, the natatorium became somewhat of a liability to the club since it was costly to maintain and constituted an additional drain on the resources of the diminishing boat club.

The Duluth Boat Club never bounced back to its former glory at the end of World War I, the way some expected. Barnes, who had brought the Duluth Boat Club to prominence through his own efforts and money, was bitterly disappointed at the way Duluthians left his own enthusiasm for the organization almost solitary. Barnes could only have concluded that it would be futile to continue trying to entice the country club crowd into supporting the Duluth Boat Club.

The club attempted to continue operating without Barnes's help for a few years, but the membership only grew smaller while the club's debts grew larger. An article in the *Duluth Herald* on January 31, 1923, told the story:

> *The Duluth Boat Club is heading into one of the biggest seasons in its history with the slimmest financial backing it ever had. Last year was a bloomer from the money side. A hard drive that was made for members was not entirely successful, and all the money that was gathered into the strong box had to be used to keep up the general high expenses of the club.*

> *For the first time since its construction, the $75,000 natatorium at the Duluth Boat Club has been standing without heat all winter, the club finding it necessary to save the price of fuel.*

CHAPTER 4: DECLINE AND FALL

Other ordinary expenditures have either been wiped out or curtailed to a minimum.

Julius Barnes, that grand gentleman, who has for many years smilingly produced the lucre to keep the financial wheels of the organization well oiled, often digging deep into his jeans for large sums, has come to the conclusion that Duluth people are not sufficiently interested in the club to support it adequately, and he cannot reasonably see why he should carry the burden of the expense single-handedly.[5]

While Barnes gave up hope for the boat club in general, his devotion to rowing remained constant. Barnes stated that he was still willing to pay the costs of any major regatta that the club proposed to enter.[6]

Cutting expenses was not a measure that could save the club. The reduced expenditures only made the club less appealing, and the number of members declined even further. Finally, on October 15, 1926, the *Christian Science Monitor* announced in headlines "Famous Duluth Boat Club Will Soon Be Dissolved." The paper went on to say:

The Duluth Boat Club, a leader in the sports and social activities of the city since its organization forty years ago, whose crews have spread the fame of the Zenith City to the four corners of the earth, will be closed and its property sold to the public.[7]

The president of the Duluth Boat Club, B. D. Ramsey, wrote to Barnes and informed him that the membership had dropped to two hundred and that the club was considerably in debt. For once, Barnes did not come to the boat

Freighter Entering Duluth-Superior Harbor. Lift Bridge Raised

When the aerial bridge was converted from a horizontal gondola to a lift bridge in 1928, it provided far easier vehicle access to and from Park Point, but it came too late to save the Duluth Boat Club.

Postcard image provided by Jerry Paulson http://www.duluth-mn-usa.com/

club's rescue. "Mr. Barnes, regretting the fact that the people of Duluth no longer have an interest in the club and its traditions, agrees that the only step open to the membership is to close the institution and sell the properties."[8]

While the story of the Duluth Boat Club itself ends here, the attempts to operate the club property as a public facility are interesting. The city did not automatically take over the Duluth Boat Club. Julius Barnes asked that the natatorium, which he donated, be returned to him.[9] He, in fact, ended up with control of all the boat club property, which he wished to sell to the City of Duluth.

Some municipal leaders, particularly Mayor Snively, did advocate purchasing the boat club facilities, but support was far from unanimous. The proposal to take over the old boat club was under consideration for two years, but the opposition was effective. They maintained that since the boat club was unable to pay operating costs by charging for its use, the city was likely to encounter the same problem, which would necessitate that the facilities be maintained by city funds, which were not in abundance during this period. Many felt that the boat club was a needless extravagance that would constitute an additional drain on the city.[10]

One objection to the purchase of the boat club property had been that it was rather difficult to reach by automobile. By 1928, this particular objection carried less validity since plans had been made to replace the old aerial bridge, which was in essence a horizontal gondola, with a lift bridge. This would give easy access to Minnesota Point by both streetcar and automobile. So, in 1928, the takeover of the boat club by the City of Duluth seemed more feasible than it had previously.

Julius Barnes was asking $90,000 for the boat club property, which in 1926 was estimated to have a depreciated value of $156,523.52 and a replacement value of $208,555.15. Barnes did not insist that the city buy the property outright, but offered to rent the property and facilities to the city for three years at 9 percent of the agreed purchase price, with an option to buy, in which case, the money paid in rent would apply to the price of the property.[11]

The city never, at any time, made plans to operate these facilities as the boat club had. There were no intentions to bring back the rowing program as Barnes had set it up, nor did the city intend to have canoes, rowboats, sailboats, and motor launches available for public use. The city was primarily interested in the natatorium, which remained one of the best swimming facilities in the nation. It was intended that the natatorium would be a self-sustaining operation, with the public being charged daily for admission. The cafés and dance halls were to be rented out. It was also proposed that either a hydroplane or seaplane dock be constructed, which would supposedly bring the city further revenue. It was thought by some that the six hundred feet of harbor frontage, which was part of the boat club property, had many commercial possibilities that the city could take advantage of.[12]

Opposition to municipal ownership of the Duluth Boat Club property was led by the West Duluth Commercial Club, which maintained that the proposed purchase of the Duluth Boat Club property had "all the appearances of a plan to open the city treasury for wasteful extravagance." A special committee of the West Duluth Commercial Club declared that the entire property was useless for any purpose, that the buildings were far gone, that the dock timbers were rotting away, that the foundations were sinking, that the eleven lots fronting the bay were valueless as dock property, and that it would require at least $100,000 to make the property usable for the purposes proposed.[13]

Apparently, the views of the West Duluth Commercial Club were convincing since Barnes's offer was not accepted by the city council, contrary to the advice of the newspapers, the mayor, and other city leaders.

In 1929, Barnes made the City of Duluth another offer. The city would assume control of the boat club property for one year, for an annual rent of one dollar. After renting the property for a year at one dollar, the city would have an option to purchase or they could rent the property again, but this time, the rent would be more substantial, as under the terms of the earlier proposal. In return, the city was to spend about $2,000 putting the property into condition. Any revenue derived from the operation would be used to pay operating expenses. The city was entitled to return the property, being under no obligation to purchase.[14]

Since there were few arguments against renting the boat club facilities for one dollar, the city council did accept Barnes's offer for the year 1930. The only activity sponsored by the city was swimming, and, apparently, it was a success, since the natatorium was visited by 20,567 people, who paid for the swimming privilege during the summer months.[15]

Despite the fact that the first season of city operation of the boat club was somewhat successful and that money was invested in some permanent improvements, the members of the city council decided that the club could not be operated under the second part of the agreement, whereby the city was to pay $8,000 in rent for the club facilities the second year, with an option to purchase within a three-year period. The city council declared that unless Barnes would allow the city to utilize the boat club under the same terms as 1930, with a rental fee of one dollar per year, the city would have to abandon operation of the boat club.

Barnes did agree to let the city operate the boat club facilities in 1931 under the same terms as in 1930. In 1931, the city expanded its operations somewhat. The Duluth Water Sports Center had rowboats and canoes available as the Duluth Boat Club had, and archery, deck tennis, and horseshoes were also promoted. In addition, the natatorium was operated as it was the year before.[16]

In 1932, negotiations between the City of Duluth and Julius Barnes followed much the same course as during the previous two years. The city, once again, stated that it could not afford to operate the Water Sports Center unless Barnes was willing to let them use it for one dollar per annum. Barnes acquiesced. In 1932, there was once again competitive rowing in Duluth. Shells that had not been used since 1925 were put into action. A regatta was put on at the Water Sports Center in August, and although the regatta was smaller and less significant than past regattas, it created much excitement in Duluth. This festival made headlines on the front page of the *Duluth Herald*, which waxed nostalgic over this revival of the old regatta days. The festival included rowing races, swimming races, a diving competition, logrolling, a lifesaving exhibition, surfboat riding, and an air show staged by the Duluth Aviation Club. Julius Barnes returned to Duluth for the event as an honored guest.[17] There was much hope that this event was the start of a return to the glory days of the past.

The City of Duluth never did appropriate funds toward the purchase of the old Duluth Boat Club property. Julius Barnes continued to let the city lease the property for the nominal fee of one dollar per year. Finally, in 1936, Barnes found a renter who was able and willing to pay a more substantial amount of money. The club properties were taken over on lease and option by the newly formed Inland Waterway, Inc., which was run by Gar Wood, a nationally known speedboat racer and builder. The boat club facilities were to be used to display and sell Gar Wood cruisers and runabouts. Besides a motorboat sales quarters, a café and lounge were also operated, and there were facilities for servicing and chartering watercraft.[18] Inland Waterway did not have outstanding success with the old Duluth Boat Club property, and the buildings were soon left empty again.

Early in World War II, the natatorium and the main house became the Lakehead Yacht Basin. The buildings were merely used as shelter to store sailboats and motorboats during the winter months. One of the walls of the swimming pool was knocked out and a gate was put in to facilitate the storing of boats.[19] The natatorium is still used this way today, although the name of the organization that owns it has changed to the Lakehead Boat Basin.

There was always talk of reviving the Duluth Boat Club. Even into 1948, the *Duluth News Tribune* recorded that J. D. Mahoney and Julius Barnes appealed to a group of Kiwanis to consider returning the former Duluth Boat Club properties to their original use and restoring rowing and other water sports programs. However, these dreams received a setback when a huge fire completely destroyed the former main house of the DBC in 1951, along with sixteen watercrafts that were being stored in the building. The cause of the fire was thought to be spontaneous combustion. Since the fire leveled the building down to the water, it was difficult to establish a definite cause.[20]

The most accurate explanation as to why the Duluth Boat Club, as a private club, petered out seems to be the shift in values and living habits among the affluent people that comprised the boat club membership. However, the failure of the City of Duluth to operate the boat club facilities requires a different explanation. The answer is simply that the city was short on revenue because of an economic depression that began immediately after World War I.

The economic boom that existed in Duluth during the last two decades of the nineteenth century when the Duluth Boat Club was founded has been described in the first section of this book. This boom made Duluth one of the nation's fifty largest cities by the turn of the century, and by 1917, Duluth had more than 90,000 inhabitants.[21] But, a number of circumstances that occurred almost simultaneously brought about a complete reversal to the economic fortunes of Duluth and northern Minnesota.

The opening of the Panama Canal caused Duluth's burgeoning oriental trade to disappear as transcontinental rail shipment ceased to be competitive. Once the Orient trade disappeared, the railroads moved their operations from Duluth to Saint Paul and Minneapolis. Railroads, in general, reached their peak in 1920, and their role in the economy of the nation declined because of the growing use of truck and air transportation.[22] The newer forms of transportation never became as important to Duluth's economy as railroads had been, but then there were getting to be fewer reasons to transport goods to or from Duluth.

By the end of World War I, Minnesota had been stripped of its pine timber, and the lumber industry was almost finished. It was coincidental that there was also an agricultural depression that began right after World War I and continued throughout the 1920s and 1930s, which affected the Northwest more severely than any other section of the country. Grain prices were low, and the value of their shipments was far less than previously recorded. At the same time, expansion of mining operations on the Mesabi Iron Range ended.[23] This is not to say that production declined, because this did not happen until after World War II, but there was not much new investment of capital. The industries that made Duluth prosperous during the heydays of the Duluth Boat Club had faded.

Duluth's economic downturn extended even past the Great Depression, perhaps because the natural resources of northeastern Minnesota were exploited by great corporations headquartered elsewhere rather than developed by locals. In contrast, the Twin Cities had their milling, timber, and railroad industries founded by local entrepreneurs who reinvested their money in the same area. They were also taking profits from the timber and railroad operations in Duluth and channeling them into Twin City enterprises. Mainly eastern industrialists and corporations owned the other major industries in the Duluth area—mining, steel production, and maritime commerce. Few of these profits were channeled back into the Duluth economy.[24]

In view of the severity and nature of the economic depression in Duluth, it is understandable that the City of Duluth could not fund the Duluth Boat Club as a part of their already large municipal park system.

1. DBC Memo, n.d., J. D. Mahoney Scrapbook, Duluth Boat Club records, NEMHC S3009.

2. Letter to DBC members from Julius H. Barnes, April 25, 1916, J. D. Mahoney Scrapbook, Duluth Boat Club records, NEMHC S3009.

3. DBC Log 1917, vol. 3, no. 3, Duluth Boat Club records, NEMHC S3009.

4. DBC Memo, n.d., J. D. Mahoney Scrapbook, Duluth Boat Club records, NEMHC S3009.

5. *Duluth Herald*, January 31, 1923, p. 17.

6. Ibid.

7. *Christian Science Monitor*, October 15, 1926, clipping, Duluth Boat Club records, Duluth Public Library.

8. Ibid.

9. Ibid.

10. *Duluth Herald*, October 13, 1928, clipping, Duluth Boat Club records, NEMHC S3009.

11. *Duluth News Tribune*, August 23, 1929, clipping, Duluth Boat Club records, NEMHC S3009.

12. *Duluth Herald*, September 11, 1928, clipping, Duluth Boat Club records, NEMHC S3009.

13. *Duluth Herald*, October 13, 1928, clipping, Duluth Boat Club records, NEMHC S3009.

14. Ibid.

15. *Duluth News Tribune*, September 12, 1930, clipping, Duluth Boat Club records, NEMHC S3009.

16. *Duluth Herald*, September 12, 1930, clipping, Duluth Boat Club records, NEMHC S3009.

17. Letter to the citizens of Duluth from the Duluth Water Sports Center (formerly the DBC), May 23, 1931, Duluth Boat Club records, NEMHC S3009.

18. *Duluth News Tribune*, August 21, 1932, p. 1.

19. *Duluth Herald*, March 14, 1936, clipping, Duluth Boat Club records, NEMHC S3009.

20. *Duluth News Tribune*, April 15, 1948, clipping, Duluth Boat Club records, NEMHC S3009.

21. *Duluth News Tribune*, April 24, 1951, clipping, Duluth Boat Club records, NEMHC S3009.

22. Daniel J. Elazar, "Constitutional Change in a Long-Depressed Community: A Case Study of Duluth, Minnesota," *Journal of the Minnesota Academy of Sciences*, vol. 33, no. 1, 1965, p. 53.

23. Ibid., p. 54.

24. Ibid.

*NEMHC refers to the Northeast Minnesota Historical Center, archives of the St. Louis County Historical Society.

CHAPTER 5

born again
AN EPILOGUE

The demise of the Duluth Boat Club in 1926 is a sad story. However, it would be misleading and wrong to end the book on this note, because rowing and other water sports are alive and well in the city of Duluth. The current programs and facilities don't compare with the glory days of the DBC. The athletes are not invincible, but they have placed in national competition and won some big races. One Duluth rower went on to win a silver medal in the Olympics, an accomplishment that escaped the oarsmen from the "Invincible Era." Every year, hundreds of Duluthians enjoy participation in the water sports programs of the new Duluth Boat Club's constituent organizations. This is a legacy of the original Duluth Boat Club.

In 1955, the Duluth Boat Club was finally resurrected, after almost thirty years of dormancy, by a group of former rowers. The new Duluth Boat Club was for competitive rowing only. The first president of this new organization was Max Rheinberger Sr., the man who rowed in the two seat of the famous Invincible Four. The Board of Directors included several other individuals who had won national championships back in the Invincible Era.[1]

The Park Point American Legion Post purchased the property at the old Oatka Branch and donated it to the Duluth Boat Club for use as a boathouse for rowing. The start was low-key. The magnificent fleet of rowing shells that the old DBC once had was gone. The new club sent out inquiries around the region looking for used rowing equipment that could be purchased inexpensively. The Duluth Boat Club rejoined the Northwestern International Rowing Association and the National Association of Amateur Oarsmen.[2]

Coach Henning Peterson (upper right) with his Duluth crew who won a junior race at the Labor Day Regatta in Saint Paul.

Photograph from the Minnesota Boat Club historical photograph collection. ND

104

CHAPTER 5: BORN AGAIN: AN EPILOGUE

Among the former champion oarsmen who helped restart the Duluth Boat Club was Henning E. Peterson, known to all as "Pete." Pete was one of the first coaches of the new Duluth Boat Club and soon became the only coach. Pete taught the sport of rowing four hours of every evening April through September until his death in 1972.

During most of the Henning Peterson era, rowing had changed very little from the Invincible Era fifty years previous. Boats and oars were still made of wood, and it was a sport primarily for young adult men. However, some big changes in the sport were just beginning to take place.

In 1967, a group of young women took the initiative of forming a rowing team in what was previously an all-male club. This group of young women trained enthusiastically and consistently beat the other fledgling women's crews in the Midwest. In 1968, they became the first Duluth team to compete for a national championship since the club was reorganized in 1955. They took fourth place in the eight in the finals of the fourth women's national rowing championships.

The Duluth Boat Club women's crew poses for a photo before leaving to compete in the fourth annual Women's National Rowing Championships in Philadelphia in 1968. From left, Bobbie Wiesen, Pam Hudson, Coach Henning Peterson, Darlene Peterson, Cathy Pharis, Mary Jo Wiesen (coxswain), Peggy Berger, Jeanne Pfeffer, Barb Dillon, Pat Hudson.

Duluth News Tribune *sports photo*

In the center, Walter Hoover (left) and Coach John Crist (right) look at the manuscript written in 1972, which is the foundation for this book. They are surrounded by Duluth Boat Club rowers who met the famous Walter Hoover when he returned to Duluth to be inducted into the Duluth Sports Hall of Fame in 1973.

Duluth News Tribune *photo by Charles Curtis*

national championships and the world stage

During the 1970s, the Duluth Boat Club became far more competitive in rowing, winning many races at the Northwestern International Regatta at all levels, and competing at the elite level. In 1978, the Duluth Boat Club officially changed its name to the Duluth Rowing Club to reflect its sole focus on the sport of rowing.

During the 1970s, one of the strongest rowers in the upper Midwest was Duluth's Dave Krmpotich. The saga of Dave Krmpotich's rowing career would make a great book in itself and cannot be adequately addressed here. Dave started rowing as a fifteen-year-old high school student. He was a key part of some fast fours and eights that won for a number of years at the Northwestern International Regatta and competed at the national level. He was infected with stories about the Invincible Era of the old Duluth Boat Club and developed a goal in life to win an Olympic medal in rowing, which is one honor that never came to the old-timers.

Although Duluth had developed one of the strongest rowing programs in the Midwest, there was no Julius Barnes to bring the program to the next level. To pursue his dream of rowing in elite competition, Dave transferred to the University of Wisconsin and made the varsity eight in his first and only season at the school. After rowing at Wisconsin, Dave moved to Philadelphia and joined the Pennsylvania Athletic Club, which was the premier club rowing program in the country. Coached by Ted Nash, Dave was a member of the U.S. national rowing team in 1979, '81, '82, '83, '85, '86, '87, '88, and '91.[3] It was in 1988 that Dave and his teammates from Penn AC won the right to represent the United States in the straight four at the Olympic Games in Seoul, South Korea, and succeeded in winning the silver medal.

CHAPTER 5: BORN AGAIN: AN EPILOGUE

Tom Perry and Dan Bryant won the Elite Lightweight Pair and Intermediate Heavyweight Pair events at the U.S. National Rowing Championships in 1977. These were the first national championships won by Duluth Rowers in more than fifty years.

Duluth News Tribune *photo by Joey McLeister*

Dave and his brother Jim Krmpotich currently coach rowing at Monsignor Bonner High School. In 2007, their team was third in the nation in high school boys eights. Dave is still rowing, and he was in the Penn AC master's eight that finished first at the Head of the Charles Regatta in 2007.

Dave Krmpotich is the best example of a Duluth rower who has left and gone on to win national championships and other elite races and has later given back to the sport through coaching. However, there are many more rowers (both men and women) who got their start at the Duluth Rowing Club and went on to row on college varsity crew teams or to win medals at the American Rowing Championships or the Canadian Henley. As an example, Dan Ringsred and Owen McVann both won races at the Canadian Henley while rowing with other clubs. Both ended up in Milwaukee where they coached high school rowers including Chris Ahrens, who went on to win a collegiate national championship in the varsity eight at Princeton, later stroked the U.S. Eight to three successive world championships, and finished his career with a gold medal in the eight at the 1994 Olympics. Owen McVann is currently head women's rowing coach at Marquette University in Milwaukee. The legacy and influence of the Duluth Boat Club continues far and wide.

The United States four without coxswain racing at the 1988 Olympic games in Seoul, South Korea. Crewmembers, from left, are Richard Kenelley, Dave Krmpotich, Tom Bohrer, and Raul Rodriguez. The United States won the silver medal in this race behind the winning East German crew and ahead of the four from West Germany.

Photo provided by Dave Krmpotich.

Above: Al Denman (left) and Pete Olson win the lightweight intermediate double at the 1993 American Rowing Championships. At this same championship regatta, Jeff Ellison and Al Denman combined with Chip Magid and John Dundon from the Minneapolis Rowing Club to win the senior quad. The Duluth Rowing Club also finished second in the men's eight dash and third in the men's intermediate eight.

Photo by Sport Graphics.

Left: The 1988 United States Olympic team selected Dave Krmpotich to be the torchbearer to represent the United States in the opening ceremonies for the 1988 Olympic games. This honor was in recognition of Dave's long rowing career that required immense perseverance to become an Olympian.

Photo provided by Dave Krmpotich.

CHAPTER 5: BORN AGAIN: AN EPILOGUE

erging (indoor rowing)

Since the 1800s, rowers have used mechanical rowing machines to train indoors during the off-season. The resistance for these machines was generally provided by hydraulics. In 1980, Dick and Pete Dreissigacker invented a rowing machine that operated with a wooden handle attached with a bicycle chain to a bike wheel and an odometer that measured performance, which made them a type of ergometer. These machines became popular across the world as excellent fitness machines, and the performance measurement gave rise to competition. Also in 1980, a group of former U.S. Olympic and World Team athletes, who called themselves the Charles River All-Star Has-Beens, started the first CRASH-B Sprints ergometer competition in Boston. Within a few short years, CRASH-B grew into the international world indoor rowing championships, which now attracts thousands of competitors from around the world.[4]

In 2000, the Duluth Rowing Club's Pete Olson won a world indoor rowing championship at the CRASH–B Sprints in the lightweight division for men between forty and fifty years of age. Pete placed second in the world the year before in this same division. His winning time for the 2000-meter race was 6 minutes and 31.8 seconds.

The winner of the world indoor rowing championships has traditionally been awarded a hammer because in rowing jargon a "hammer" is a rower who has enormous strength and little finesse with the blades. Indoor rowing does not require the finesse of rowing on the water. This is the hammer and medal won by Pete Olson at the 2000 CRASH-B Sprints.

Photograph by Bruce Ojard Photographics

109

Dan O'Neill races at the FISA World Master's Regatta in Vienna, Austria, in 1993, where he won four gold medals. Photo provided by Dan O'Neill.

master's rowing

During the Invincible Era of the Duluth Boat Club, there was no age-categorized competitive rowing, except for occasional exhibition events. In the early 1970s, age-categorized competition for older rowers became formalized and was termed "Master's Rowing." The Duluth Rowing Club has a very strong Master's Rowing program for both men and women.

Age categories for Master's Rowing are as follows:

A—*Minimum age 27 or more*
B—*Average age 36 or more*
C—*Average age 43 or more*
D—*Average age 50 or more*
E—*Average age 55 or more*
F—*Average age 60 or more*
G—*Average age 65 or more*
H—*Average age 70 or more*

CHAPTER 5: BORN AGAIN: AN EPILOGUE

During the 1990s, the Duluth Rowing Club's Dan O'Neill was one of the top master single scullers in the world, dominating the age category for rowers thirty-six years old and older. O'Neill won the B Single championship at the Master's National Regatta in 1991 at Austin, Texas, and in 1992 at Camden, New Jersey, where he and Dave Krmpotich also won the B Double. In 1993, Dan won gold medals in both the A Single and B Single at the FISA World Rowing Master's Regatta in Vienna, Austria. He also combined with a sculler from the Ann Arbor Rowing Club to take a gold medal in the Mixed B Double and combined with Arne Lande from the Minneapolis Rowing Club to capture gold in the Men's D Double. In 1994, O'Neill won the B Single at the Master's Nationals in Augusta, Georgia. In 1995, he won the Father/Daughter Double with his daughter Erin O'Neill at the Master's Nationals in Saint Paul, Minnesota. At the 1995 Master's Nationals, a number of other Duluth rowers competed. Pete Olson won the Men's Lightweight B Single and combined with Al Denman to win the Men's Lightweight AB Double. Duluth also had four second-place finishes and a couple of third-place finishes at this regatta.

Jeff Ellison and Al Denman won the Men's AB Pair at the 1996 Master Nationals in Syracuse, New York.

Pete Olson and Al Denman also won the Lightweight AB Double championship at this same regatta.

Photo by Sports Graphics.

The Duluth Rowing Club wins the Men's B Quad at the 1999 Masters Nationals at Lake Lanier, Georgia. From left, Al Denman, Pete Olson, Joe Kormann, and Troy Howell. At the same regatta, Al Denman combined with Jeff Ellison to win the Men's B Pair and teamed with Pete Olson to win the Men's Lightweight B Double. Denman, Olson, Kormann, and Ellison also won the Men's B Coxed Four, coxed by Jocelyn Rheinholdt. In addition, Duluth took two silver medals and a bronze at the 1999 Master's Nationals.

Photo provided by Joe Kormann.

The Duluth Rowing Club Master's team at the Canadian Master's National Championships in Kenora, Ontario, in 2002. The DRC took firsts in Men's AB Four, Men's C Four, Men's C Double, Mixed C-H Eight, Men's C-H Eight, and Mixed C-D Quad, and second in the Men's C-D Quad and Men's AB Double.

Photographer unknown.

Above: National Championship (U.S. and Canadian) medals won by Pete Olson in the course of his rowing career with the Duluth Rowing Club (so far). There are a number of Duluth rowers with a similar pile of medals.

Photograph by Bruce Ojard Photographics

The Duluth Rowing Club C Four wear their gold medals at the FISA World Rowing Masters Regatta in Montreal, Canada, in 2001. From left, Jeff Ellison, Pete Olson, Mike Cochran, and Al Denman. Ellison and Cochran teamed with Dan O'Neil and Gary White to win a gold medal in the Men's D Quad, while Ellison and Denman won gold in the Men's B Pair.

Photo by Emily Cochran.

INVINCIBLE: HISTORY OF THE DULUTH BOAT CLUB

Rowers at the start of the women's junior eight race at the Duluth International Regatta in 1999. The Duluth Rowing Club team (second from the top) pulled ahead to win by two lengths open water. Team members were Molly Cochran, Savannah Malone, Alex Holter, Alice Christenson, Jodi Baumgarth, Lauren Baker, Jenna Munson, Wendy Johnson, and coxswain Chris Voltzke.

Duluth News Tribune *staff photo by Josh Biggs*

Even into the 1970s, high school rowers (like Greg Peterson and Dan Ringsred shown here making some wash) were competing against older rowers since there wasn't a competitive division for rowers eighteen and under.

Photo provided by Greg Peterson.

CHAPTER 5: BORN AGAIN: AN EPILOGUE

DRC junior four shown after winning at the 2007 Northwestern International Regatta in Regina, Saskatchewan. From left, Aaron Matuseski, Scott Grindy, Jonathon Halquist, Ben Ellison, and coxswain Jenna Proctor.

Photo by Jane Bertani

junior rowing

In addition to age-restricted competition for older rowers, another change from the old days is a rowing category for younger rowers eighteen years old and younger, which is termed junior rowing. In the old days, a junior rower was a rower who had not won a qualifying race to advance to the next level, and it had nothing to do with age. Current DRC head coach Bonnie Fuller-Kask has been instrumental in developing the Duluth Rowing Club junior program to the point where an average of more than seventy boys and girls participate annually. Nearly every year, several of them go on to row in college.

Death Row

During the early 1980s, Duluth rowers began rowing up the St. Louis River from Park Point to Fond du Lac, a distance of 25,000 meters. It wasn't long before some rowers from the Minnesota Boat Club joined in, and within a few years, this leisurely distance row morphed into an annual racing event affectionately known as "Death Row." This race is distinctive because the event is open to an unlimited number of boats and there is a mass start stretching across St. Louis Bay. In fact, the *2008–2009 Rower's Almanac* listed Death Row as one of the ten most unique rowing races in the nation.

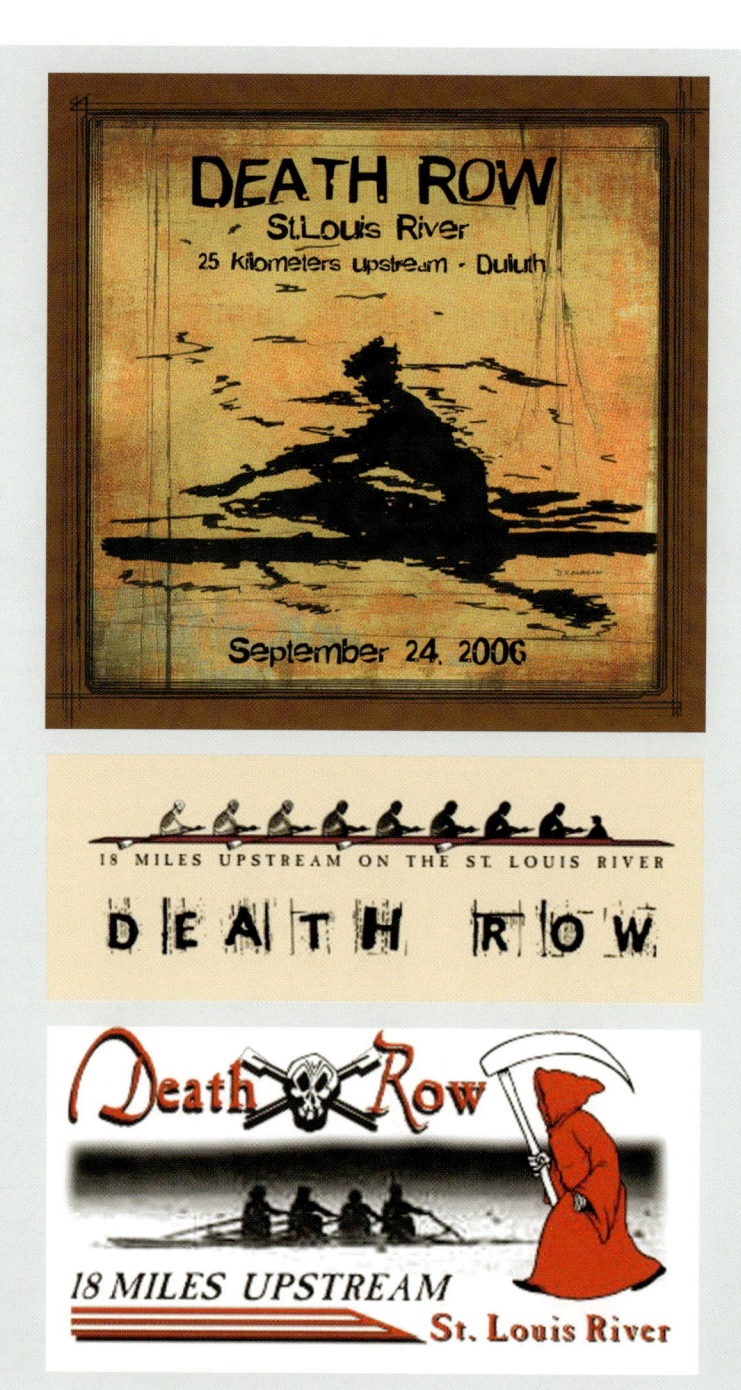

Minneapolis Eight on their way to setting the course record for Eights at Death Row in a time of 1:39:40 in 2003.

Duluth News Tribune *staff photo by Clint Austin*

Duluth Rowing Club junior boys quad members Jake Boyce (left) and Zach Ellison during the 2003 Death Row.

Duluth News Tribune *staff photo by Clint Austin*

The University of Minnesota Eight breaking the course record for Eights at Death Row in 2006.

Photo by Jim Forsberg

INVINCIBLE: HISTORY OF THE DULUTH BOAT CLUB

duluth regatta

The Duluth Rowing Club annually hosts the Duluth International Regatta, which is one of the largest rowing events in the upper Midwest. Here is a selection of photos from the Duluth Regatta over the years.

Dan Bryant, winner of the Men's Open Single Race in 1978.
Duluth News Tribune *photo by Joey McLeister*

Julie Scott and Leah Olson win the women's junior pair in 1992.
Duluth News Tribune *staff photo by Clara Wu*

Nancy LaTour and Cathy Dowhus compete in the women's double in 1988.
Duluth News Tribune *photo by Steve Stearns taken July 23, 1988.*

Bonnie Fuller Kask (left), Claire Smith, Craig Lincoln, and Paul Diedrich of the Duluth Rowing Club try to stay ahead of a team from Thunder Bay in the mixed master's quad race of the Duluth International Regatta in 2004.

Duluth News Tribune *staff photo by Justin Hayworth*

Dan O'Neill (left), Jeff Ellison, Pete Olson, and Al Denman get focused for the open quad race in 1991. Dan O'Neill won the open single at this regatta while Jeff Ellison and Al Denman won the open pair race.

Duluth News Tribune *photo by Clara Wu taken July 20, 1991.*

head racing

Another type of rowing competition that came into being after the Invincible Era is head racing. Head races are usually on rivers with a large number of competitors that row one race (usually three miles in distance) against the clock with each crew starting one at a time. The Duluth Rowing Club participates in a number of different head races: the Head of the Mississippi, the Head of the Rock, the Milwaukee River Challenge (two miles upstream and two miles downstream), the Head of the Iowa, and the famous Head of the Charles Regatta in Boston, Massachusetts.

Duluth Rowing Club competes at the 2006 Head of the Charles in the men's senior master eights (average age fifty-plus). From left, coxswain Erica Robertson, Greg Peterson, Tom Rauschenfels, Pete Olson, Andrew Slade, Mike Cochran, Dave Kask, Kurt Fox, and Glen Nordehn.

Photo by Sports Graphics

The DRC Women's master four competes at the 2002 Head of the Charles Regatta. From the top in bow, Claire Smith, Bonnie Fuller-Kask, Sarah Faltinson, Gretchen Madsen, and coxswain Chris Voltzke. Photo by Sport Graphics. This crew finished fourth out of twenty-five teams entered in the event. In 2006, Gretchen Madsen combined with three women from the Minneapolis Rowing Club to win the Women's Senior Master Four at the Head of the Charles.

Photo by Sports Graphics

Greg Peterson and Tom Rauschenfells compete in the 2007 senior master double race at the Head of the Charles Regatta.

Photo by Sports Graphics

CHAPTER 5: BORN AGAIN: AN EPILOGUE

name confusion

In the late 1990s, the Duluth Rowing Club Board of Directors decided to partner with other water sports organizations to develop a community water sports center. In 1999, the venerable name of the Duluth Boat Club came back once again to describe an umbrella organization for the Duluth Rowing Club, Duluth-Superior Sailing Association, the Duluth Yacht Club, and Courage Duluth. The Duluth Boat Club has also developed its own paddling programs, having acquired several kayaks, two outrigger canoes, and a dragon boat that was donated by Harbortown Rotary Club.

The Duluth Yacht Club hosts a series of races every Wednesday night throughout the summer; some races take place on Lake Superior while others are held on St. Louis Bay.

Photos by Clint Austin

121

Duluth-Superior Sailing Association provides an opportunity for Harbor City International School students to practice their sailing skills on Superior Bay.

Duluth News Tribune *photo by Derek Neas, June 3, 2003*

The Duluth Boat Club is a key partner in the Lake Superior Dragon Boat Festival, which is organized by the Rotary Club of Superior and the Duluth Harbortown Rotary Club. This festival attracts more than eighty twenty-two-person teams every year and annually raises well over $100,000 for charitable causes.

Photo provided by the Lake Superior Dragon Boat Festival.

Spinnakers try to catch every little puff of wind as sailboats compete in the San Juan 24 North American Sailing Championships on Lake Superior, July 26, 2002.

Duluth News Tribune *photo by Derek Neas*

Duluth Boat Club

The Duluth Boat Club vision is to provide a community water sports center for the programs of its affiliate organizations. This building elevation designed by Helstrom Architects brings back a lot of the ambience and class of the Duluth Boat Club in its glory days.

A laser sailboat race hosted by Duluth-Superior Sailing Association.

Photo provided by Duluth Community Sailing.

Courage Duluth, in partnership with the Duluth Boat Club, also provides a paddling program. The individuals in this photo are participant Reid Hietala in the foreground, volunteer Craig Lincoln in the stern of the kayak, and Claire Krebs, Courage Participant, in the bow.

Photo provided by Courage Duluth.

Dragon boat racing is very much like the war canoe racing from the glory years, except that the heritage is Chinese instead of Native American. Dragon boating is one of the fastest growing competitive water sports in the world.

Photo provided by the Lake Superior Dragon Boat Festival.

Sailing in the Norlin Mark III 2.4 meter sailboat is Sam Tabaka, Courage Center participant. The boat, owned by Courage Duluth, is especially designed for people with physical disabilities. Courage Duluth provides fifteen seasonal weekly community-based recreation programs and eighteen one-day special events to people of all ages and levels of physical abilities. Courage Duluth delivers its services through the efforts of more than 140 volunteers and collaboration with organizations such as the Duluth Boat Club, Duluth-Superior Sailing Association, and the Duluth Rowing Club.

Photo provided by Erik Larson, executive director of Courage Duluth.

CHAPTER 5: BORN AGAIN: AN EPILOGUE

the legacy

The network of organizations involved in the current Duluth Boat Club may not have the finest water sports facilities in the world, and its athletes are very good but not invincible. However, the current Duluth Boat Club consists of several vibrant organizations that are open to men and women of almost any age, income level, or physical ability. Even the Duluth Yacht Club considers itself a "blue collar" sailing club, and it is very easy for anyone to crew on the Duluth Yacht Club's Wednesday night races. The DBC affiliates connect to the rich heritage of the Duluth Boat Club from the glory years, but they strive to serve all community members and pride themselves on being as inclusive as the original Duluth Boat Club formed in 1886 was proudly exclusive.

Glenn Nordehn is shown hoisting the Lipton Cup, which is a trophy donated by Sir Thomas Lipton to the Winnipeg Rowing Club in 1914 in honor of the great oarsman Con Riley. The Lipton Cup is annually awarded to the club in the Northwestern International Rowing Association that accumulates the most points from all events at the annual championship regatta. Winning the Lipton Cup is a continual goal for the Duluth Rowing Club, because to win this trophy a club has to be strong in all categories: men, women, open, juniors, masters, sculling, and sweeping.

1. *Duluth News Tribune* clipping from May 1, 1955, NEMHC S30009 B1f2.
2. Ibid.
3. Friends of Rowing History website http://www.rowinghistory.net/US%20Team/members-k.htm.
4. http://www.crash-b.org/history.htm.

*NEMHC refers to the Northeast Minnesota Historical Center, archives of the St. Louis County Historical Society.

michael cochran

Michael Cochran has been a competitive rower since 1967, with the exception of three years active duty service overseas in the U.S. Navy. He has a B.A. in philosophy from the University of Minnesota, where he also raced in varsity competition with the U of M crew and wrote a research manuscript on the history of the Duluth Boat Club, which is the foundation for this book. Michael and his wife Diane have four adult children (James, Molly, Emily, Anna) and two grandchildren (Noah, Isabelle) and live on the banks of the St. Louis River in Duluth. For the past twenty years, their home has served as the finish line for Death Row, a unique twenty-five-kilometer rowing race.

Photo of the author by Bruce Ojard Photographics

The author rowing at the Master's National Championships in Augusta, Georgia, 1994. Photo by Sports Graphics www.sport-graphics.com